A WARRIOR'S CALLING

A WARRIOR'S CALLING
A CHALLENGE TO REAL FAITH FOR GUYS

Jeremy V. Jones
Greg Asimakoupoulos

SERIES CREATED BY
MICHAEL ROSS

Editor: Marianne Hering
Cover design and photos: Jeff Lane/brandango.us
Model: Broadmoor Talent Agency

ISBN 10: 1-58997-343-7
ISBN 13: 978-1-58997-343-5

Printed in the United States of America
1 2 3 4 5 6 7 8 9 / 12 11 10 09 08 07 06

To all the guys who make up
the *Breakaway* nation:

"Friends, don't get me wrong: By no means
do I count myself an expert in all of this,
but I've got my eye on the goal, where God
is beckoning us onward — to Jesus. I'm off
and running, and I'm not turning back. So
let's keep focused on that goal, those of us
who want everything God has for us"
(Philippians 3:13-15, *The Message*). –J. V. J.

I dedicate this book to my personal tribe (all
female warriors). To my wife, Wendy, and my
three daughters, Kristin, Allison, and Lauren
Star. The four of you fuel my desire to live a
life of extreme devotion. I love you. –G. A.

CONTENTS

INTRODUCTION

Discover God's Will for Your Life!

You sit by yourself in youth group—feeling totally clueless.

Tonight's topic: "Knowing God's Will." All evening guys and girls are standing up, testifying about all the cool ways Christ is leading their lives.

"The Lord told me to study medicine after high school," an attractive girl blurts.

"God is calling me to the mission field this summer," says a boy with a surfer dude accent.

Another guy breaks into tears, then says, "Jesus wants me to give up some bad friendships. It's hard, but I know I have to do it."

Everyone applauds. You slump back in your chair and squeeze shut your eyes. *Okay, Lord. I'm missing something here. Every other teen in this room seems so clued in to what You want for their lives. NOT ME. I feel absolutely CLUELESS! Why can't I hear Your voice?*

Figuring out God's will for your life may seem overwhelming at times. It may even feel like some sort of mysterious riddle that's solved by only the holiest youth group saints. (Which completely excludes you, right?!)

Guess what. Getting a clue about God's will isn't as

hard as you think. It all boils down to *where* you look for answers and *whom* you listen to.

This book will help.

During the next few weeks . . .

- You'll gain a deeper understanding of your faith, which impacts your calling in life.

- You'll plug into the truth. You know what the Messiah did nearly 2,000 years ago—He came into the world, died on a cross, then was resurrected into heaven. And you know what that means for all who commit their lives to Him—*salvation* (eternal life), *liberation* (freedom for the captives), and *restoration* (healing of the brokenhearted).

- You'll experience a radical transformation in your heart. You'll realize that you are someone who can't possibly sit still and stay quiet about what you believe and where your life is going.

- You'll accept the mission of living your faith . . . and telling the world what it is that anchors your life.

Before you dive into these pages, let me remind you of two important facts about your faith: (1) Walking the Christian walk is often hard, yet (2) you can make it if you choose to trust Jesus and step out with an iron-willed commitment.

So what's an iron-willed commitment? Read all of Hebrews 11 and the first verses of chapter 12, then focus on the following verses:

Let us throw off everything that hinders and the sin that so easily entangles, and let us run with perseverance the race marked out for us. Let us fix our eyes on Jesus, the author and perfecter of our faith, who for the joy set before him endured the cross, scorning its shame, and sat down at the right hand of the throne of God. Consider him who endured such opposition from sinful men, so that you will not grow weary and lose heart. (Hebrews 12:1-3)

Jesus overcame death on the cross so that—through His power—each one of us can overcome the obstacles that stand in our way . . . no matter how hopeless the situation may seem.

It's this realization that has made a difference in my own walk with Jesus. Through the years, I've discovered that I'm not alone in my struggles. I've learned that every Christian, at one time or another, wrestles with various hurts and fears . . . even feelings of inadequacy. The truth is, as a Christian—as a young man who is heading down the road to eternal life—life is more often hard than easy.

But pressing on with an iron will is the key. That's what Jesus did as He went to the cross. And He overcame death and the struggles of this world just for you and me. He headed down a road that took Him to His physical death. But He also walked down a spiritual road that led to life.

He wants to take you down that life-giving road, too.

—Michael Ross

Breakaway Magazine Editor

Okay. So what exactly is this you're getting into? Is this a devotional? Is it a journal? Is it a *journey?*

Actually, yes to all of them.

In each daily entry you'll find:

- **A TRIBAL QUEST**—a faith challenge for the day.
- **A TRIBAL TRUTH**—Scripture that defines a Christian's tribal creed.
- **A TRIBAL FACE**—a true account of a teen like you, a time-proven warrior, or a Bible hero who sought after God's heart and earned himself a new identity in God's worldwide tribe.
- **TRIBAL TRAINING**—advice, action points, and thought-provoking questions and strategies for applying God's truth to your life.
- **TRIBAL MARKS**—a place to jot down your own prayers, thoughts, hopes . . . and all the new stuff you've learned.

So, don't hold back! Fulfill what burns in every young man's heart. Dare to trust your Creator and become the warrior He made you to be.

Use this life-changing resource as a way to get connected to God's eternal tribe. Study with a friend or group of guys from church—maybe even your dad (you know, as your own tribal rite-of-passage thing).

Your ultimate journey awaits. Join the adventure of following Christ. And with each quest He gives you, don't be surprised if you find yourself facing—and overcoming—challenges far greater than anything you ever imagined.

A WARRIOR'S CALLING

KNOW WHO YOU ARE
WEEK 1

SURVIVOR SECRETS

TRIBAL QUEST

Learn to see yourself as your Creator views you: a priceless masterpiece made with an important purpose.

EXPLORE THE WORD: PSALM 139:1-16

TRIBAL TRUTH

For you created my inmost being;
> *you knit me together in my mother's womb.*
I praise you because I am fearfully and wonderfully made;
> *your works are wonderful,*
I know that full well. —PSALM 139:13-14

TRIBAL FACE

Jeremiah—Young Prophet

The young Hebrew man felt the flush of embarrassment. He turned to see who had entered the courtyard and caught him talking to himself.

Puzzled, he looked around seeing no one. *I know I heard my name,* he thought. *Maybe it's that cruel Eleazar playing pranks again.*

He hoped not. Though he had grown accustomed to the teasing that came from being the son of a priest, the young man still felt the sting of the laughter at his expense. He was smart, certainly, and had always done well in his studies to become a priest like his father, Hilkiah. But he felt shy and awkward around others and was never popular in his village.

"Jeremiah," came the voice again. This time the young man was certain he heard it, but who—

"Jeremiah!"

Jeremiah's knees buckled and he fell facedown to the ground. There was no mistaking it now: This was the voice of the Lord, and it filled him with terror.

"Before I formed you in the womb I knew you, before you were born I set you apart; I appointed you as a prophet to the nations."

The young man could scarcely believe his ears. *Me? A prophet? Surely there is some mistake!*

Covering his face, he somehow managed to stammer, "Ah, sovereign Lord, I do not know how to speak; I am only a child."

The Lord's voice was firm yet compassionate. "Do not say, 'I am only a child.' You must go to everyone I send you to and say whatever I command you."

A wave of nausea swept over Jeremiah. The familiar sense of fear and embarrassment rose up within him at the mention of the task.

But God continued, "Do not be afraid of them, for I am with you and will rescue you."

A surge of hope shot through Jeremiah's heart. As God spoke, He raised Jeremiah's head from the sand and placed His hand to the young man's mouth. It felt as if flames were licking Jeremiah's lips, their heat surging deep within his spirit.

"Now, I have put my words in your mouth," God said. "See, today I appoint you over nations and kingdoms to uproot and tear down, to destroy and overthrow, to build and to plant."

With each continuing word, Jeremiah felt a strength he had never known. New confidence rose up within him as he clung to God's command. *Maybe*—

Suddenly, a vision burned in the new prophet's brain. He reached out his hand to touch it but felt empty air.

"What do you see, Jeremiah?" God said.

The man hesitated for a moment. "I . . . . I see the branch of an almond tree," he said with uncertainty.

"Very good," came the voice of the Lord. "You have seen correctly."

Again Jeremiah's mind was consumed by another vision. Again, God questioned, "What do you see?"

This time Jeremiah spoke readily. "I see a boiling pot tilting away from the north," he said.

Again God gave His approval. "From the north disaster will be poured out on all who live in the land."

Jeremiah's spirit leaped. God was pleased with *him*.

"Get yourself ready!" the Lord said and repeated His command to the man. "Today I have made you a fortified city, an iron pillar and a bronze wall to stand against the whole land—against the kings of Judah, its officials, its priests, and the people of the land. They will fight against you but will not overcome you, for I am with you and will rescue you."

The young man bowed low to the ground. God's words had seared his soul. He would never be the same.

Put yourself in Jeremiah's shoes. He probably wasn't much older than you, and maybe you can identify with his sense of uncertainty and insecurity. He was minding his own business, trying to obey God's laws and become a good priest. Then *BAM!* God revolutionized his life.

Did you catch that mission? Go tell the kings that God doesn't like what they're up to. No wonder the young Jeremiah was a bit intimidated. Who can blame him? That's big responsibility—and danger, especially in a day when the king could do just about anything (like lop off your head) if you didn't make him happy.

But God had big plans, and His call came with every-thing His young servant needed:

Significance: God's opening statements gave mean-ing to life. The Creator of the universe knew Jeremiah before he existed and had plans for him even then.

Tools: God was not concerned with Jeremiah's protests. He provided the words and everything else Jeremiah needed for the task.

Protection: "I am with you and will rescue you," the Lord said to Jeremiah. God knew this was a difficult assignment, but He promised His presence. When the Lord calls us, He doesn't leave us by ourselves.

Practice: God wasn't playing games when He asked Jeremiah what he saw. He was providing reassurance to the young prophet, sharpening his skills and clarifying His message.

Identity: Talk about encouragement! Do you think Jeremiah ever forgot the words God spoke to him that day? Jeremiah had viewed himself as a child; God declared him to be a fortress of a man who could not be harmed.

Jeremiah believed God's words and acted on them. He answered his Creator's calling, rose up, and fulfilled his mission. Thousands of years later, he is considered one of the greatest Old Testament prophets—a far cry from the timid, insecure young man he once was.

How do you see yourself? Where is your identity rooted? What is God's calling to you?

TRIBAL TRAINING

• **Get God's eyes.** Just like Jeremiah, God created you with unique and special gifts. He knew just who you would be and what purposes He had for you. In other words, you matter! Read Psalm 139:1-16. Compare your view of yourself to what God says in these verses. This is where true identity begins. Do you believe it, or, like Jeremiah, are you stuck with a warped perception of yourself? Memorize these verses and repeat them to yourself when you feel insignificant.

• **Answer the call.** God probably hasn't spoken audibly to you like He did to Jeremiah. But just because you haven't received a specific assignment from the Lord doesn't mean you won't. If God has a particular task He wants you to accomplish, rest assured He will leave no doubt about it. Even more important, God's call to each of us is first to Himself. He wants us to know Him, serve Him, represent Him, and obey His Word with everything we've got. How can you do that today? Do you sense God calling you to do something or go somewhere?

• **Do it.** Whether you've identified a specific or general calling, it's time to stand up and trust God, not yourself. Make a plan today. Take a specific action. Want to share Christ with a friend? Call and invite him to hang out. Feel like you should pursue a career as a graphic designer? Sign up for an art class at your school or a local community college. God told Jeremiah, "Get yourself ready!" (Jeremiah 1:17). You don't have to fulfill your entire calling today, but get started by taking that first step.

• **PRAY IT OUT:** *"Lord, thank You for creating and loving me. Please help me to see myself as You do and be all You desire me to be."* Thank God that He knew you before you were born. Praise Him for His creativity and wisdom in making you just the way you are. Ask Him to help you hear and follow His call for your life.

TRIBAL MARKS

A KEY POINT I LEARNED TODAY: _____

_____

_____

_____

_____

_____

_____

HOW I WANT TO GROW: _____

_____

_____

_____

_____

_____

_____

MY PRAYER LIST: _____

_____

_____

_____

_____

_____

_____

SURVIVOR SECRETS

▶▶▶**WEEKLY MEMORY VERSE:** *So God created man in his own image, in the image of God he created him; male and female he created them.* —**GENESIS 1:27**

TRIBAL QUEST

When faced with the temptation to fit in, you don't need to become a hostage to fear and compromise.

EXPLORE THE WORD: GALATIANS 3:26–4:7

TRIBAL TRUTH

Because you are sons, God sent the Spirit of his Son into our hearts, the Spirit who calls out, "Abba, Father." So you are no longer a slave, but a son; and since you are a son, God has made you also an heir. —**GALATIANS 4:6-7**

TRIBAL FACE

A Teen Guy Overcomes Peer Fear

FICTION BY GREG ASIMAKOUPOULOS

Manny's most memorable ceremony was the day he was baptized at his grandma's church. But tonight, something else would come close to equaling its status.

When he was 10 years old, Manny

had understood how much God loved him and publicly professed faith in Jesus. His parents and his brother, Victor, were not believers, but his dad's mom was. She had told him Bible stories since he was a toddler. And every time he spent the weekend with her, he went to church with her. It was on one such weekend when he told the pastor he wanted to be baptized.

Manny thought about that day a lot. A snapshot he kept in his Bible reminded him of it. It was a photo his grandma took of him standing next to her pastor in the middle of the river that flowed by the rural church. His dark-skinned face stood out against the bright white baptismal robe. He could still feel the warm sun and the cold water.

He also could feel an awesome sense of acceptance that day. As he came up out of the water and struggled to catch his breath, the congregation smiled and clapped enthusiastically. A few women his grandma's age even shouted "Hallelujah!"

That was five years ago. Although Manny was still taking his young faith seriously, he was about to experience something he anticipated would be almost as awesome. Ever since his older brother, Victor, joined the Stallions, he knew he wanted to be part of this gang, because unlike most of the gangs in Albuquerque, New Mexico, the Stallions were known as a nonviolent organization. Manny had no interest in crime or hurting people.

Those who belonged to the Stallions were proud of being Mexican-American. They wore black leather jackets with an insignia of a galloping steed on the back. The gang hung together every Friday and Saturday night. They were like family. And for most of those in the Stallions, a sense of belonging was important. Almost all of the boys were from homes without fathers.

In order to join the gang you had to be sponsored by a Stallion and you had to be 15 years old. Victor, who was four years older than Manny, told him he would be his sponsor once he turned the minimum age. And that day had arrived.

At school that day, Manny could hardly concentrate as he envisioned the initiation ceremony that night. He would soon cross the threshold of masculinity. Tonight he would be accepted by the Stallions as a Stallion.

Victor picked up his brother in his sleek, black, low-riding Prelude. Manny greeted him with a high five and a big smile. Together they drove 20 miles out of town to an abandoned gas station on a dirt road. Thirty gang members were already there wearing black jackets and blue jeans.

While the Stallions circled Manny, one gang member handed the young recruit a pistol and told him to shoot a rattlesnake that another member let loose from a burlap sack. The snake coiled and made its signature sound. But Manny took aim and shot the slithering target through the head, leaving it lifeless in the desert sand. The 15-year-old felt a rush of excitement as the gang cheered its approval.

"Before we present you with your black jacket, you still have another task to perform to prove you are worthy of being a Stallion," the leader of the gang said. "Please remove your clothes except for your underpants."

As Manny complied with their odd request, he was led by two gang members to the rusted-out old-fashioned gas pump. A third Stallion blindfolded him. A fourth tied him with rope. With that, the group got into their cars and began to peel out. He heard his brother's voice above the sound of the modified exhaust systems. "We'll be back to get you for breakfast."

Manny couldn't really sleep in a standing position tied to the pumps. To make matters worse, he nearly froze. His feet and hands were numb with the poor circulation caused from the rope and with the desert cold. He tried to convince himself he wasn't afraid as he heard distant coyotes and the eerie sound of desert owls. He was nervous; sweat beaded over his entire body, generating even worse chills as it cooled. Wearing a blindfold, he couldn't tell when the sun had come up, yet he could feel warm rays on his unclothed chest. His eyes teared up, but with joy not fear. When he heard the sound of cars and voices, he breathed a sigh of relief.

"We'll present your black jacket at breakfast," the gang leader said as he removed the rope and black fabric that had covered his face. "Get dressed and let's go get some food."

Victor drove Manny while the other cars followed in caravan style.

"Where do we have breakfast?" Manny asked his brother.

"We'll stop to get the food and meet the gang down the road at a park," Victor explained.

Just then Victor pulled into a convenience store. "Here's a list of what we need. Bread, cold cuts, sodas, chips. And you'll need this since we don't have any money."

Victor handed his brother the pistol he'd used to kill the snake.

"This is your last test, little brother," Victor said with a twinkle in his eye. "I know you won't let us down."

Manny felt sick inside. The Stallions were just like the rest of the local gangs after all. Violent. Cruel.

He also felt something else. It was the Holy Spirit prompting him to not give in to peer pressure. Throwing the gun on the floorboard of his brother's car, he opened the door and started to run.

"I won't do it," he yelled. "I'm not turning my back on what is right just to be a Stallion."

As you might guess, there are all kinds of reasons why guys like Manny want to be accepted and belong. And when we long for love, we can find ourselves vulnerable to joining the wrong crowd.

Even Christians are tempted to close their eyes to compromising situations in order to fit in. But the Lord never turns His back on those who belong to Him. He puts a desire in their hearts to take a stand and turn away when necessary.

TRIBAL TRAINING

• **Expect temptations when you track with the pack.** The battle with peer pressure is not unique to the teenage years. It's a battle we fight all our lives. When we anticipate it, it becomes less scary, especially

if we begin our day thanking God we are part of a forever family.

• **Remind yourself of your position in Christ.**
When you feel ostracized, thank God you're not alone. As
a Christian you have been adopted into the family of
God. When you accepted Jesus as your Savior and Lord
you were given rights and privileges of a son of God.
Whenever you start a prayer with "Father," stop and
think how cool it is that you can call Him that.

• **Prioritize time with other Christians.** Hebrews
10:25 says, "Let us not give up meeting together, as
some are in the habit of doing, but let us encourage one
another." In other words, be intentional about who you
spend the most time with. You are less likely to cave in
to those who don't take God seriously if you are hanging
with those who do.

• **PRAY IT OUT:** *"Lord, I need Your help to resist the
crowd and do what is right."* Confess to the Lord what
you are tempted to do in order to be accepted by your
friends. Ask Him for the courage to say no when you
need to.

TRIBAL MARKS

A KEY POINT I LEARNED TODAY: _____

_____

_____

_____

_____

_____

_____

HOW I WANT TO GROW: _____

_____

_____

_____

_____

_____

MY PRAYER LIST: _____

_____

_____

_____

_____

_____

_____

SURVIVOR SECRETS

>>>**WEEKLY MEMORY VERSE:** *So God created man in his own image, in the image of God he created him; male and female he created them.* —**GENESIS 1:27**

TRIBAL QUEST

When you take stock in the unique abilities and interests God has given you, celebrate the fact they're for a purpose.

EXPLORE THE WORD: EPHESIANS 2:1-10

TRIBAL TRUTH

For we are God's workmanship, created in Christ Jesus to do good works, which God prepared in advance for us to do. —**EPHESIANS 2:10**

TRIBAL FACE

Matthew—A Jewish Tax Collector

Pardon the pun, but Matthew's occupation was a taxing career.

Sitting in an open-air booth could be very draining during the summer months for Matthew. But enduring the intense heat wasn't the half of it. Enduring the sarcastic (and even cruel) comments of his fellow citizens was even more stifling.

Yes, Matthew was Jewish, but he worked for the Roman government. His job required him to collect taxes from other Jews in order to fund Caesar's rather elaborate lifestyle. If you think the government takes more than its share when your parents fill out their tax return for the Internal Revenue Service, you wouldn't believe what Rome required the citizens of Israel to cough up. It was no wonder the Jews hated people like Matthew. He was considered a traitor. And since he was a Jew, he was hated by his Roman employers, too.

But in addition to being hated, Matthew was also pretty well-off. Scratch that. He was quite well-off. The dude was rich. Many years earlier he'd made peace with the fact that he wasn't going to have friends (except other tax collectors), so he decided he'd have a comfy life.

Based on what the Bible tells us, Matthew's base of operation was near the Sea of Galilee. It's likely it was right on the main highway that connected Persia with Egypt. That's where he was when Jesus encountered him.

"Hey, Mr. Tax Man!" Jesus probably probed. "What's your name?"

At first Matthew ignored the question. Nobody ever asked him a question expecting an answer, except maybe one like, "Do you know how much people hate you?"

"Matthew, my name is Matthew," the wealthy untouchable replied.

Matthew knew what his name in Hebrew meant. "Gift of the Lord." What a joke. The name his mother gave him as a baby wasn't anything close to how he felt about himself. He wasn't a gift of the Lord. As far as his Jewish associates felt, he was a jerk. Perhaps Matthew was rolling in the bucks, but he was lonely as heck. He struggled with guilt. And for good reason. He'd gouged people every day of his life for as long as he could remember in order to feather his comfortable nest.

But Jesus wasn't going to let Matthew off the hook that easily. He was convinced that this spiritually poor rich man could reach a point in his life where he would really see his life as a gift.

"Matthew?" the carpenter-turned-rabbi said. "Come with Me. Leave your table of injustice and let Me teach you a new career."

Matthew must have been ready for that kind of invitation. It's obvious he wasn't happy with his life. Even without asking what Jesus had in mind, Matthew dropped the canvas flap on his tentlike booth, closed up shop, and made tracks in the hot sand to catch up with the Teacher. Heck, he didn't even take the velvet bags of coins that were left heaped under his table.

Whatever Jesus saw in Matthew, his invitation to join the other disciples was something Matthew found irresistible. The well-dressed tax man in the expensive threads and manicured beard left his livelihood behind. He started hanging with fishermen whose robes smelled like trout.

Before the week was out, Matthew planned a party for his friends. You guessed it. They were tax collectors just like him. He spread the word. "YOU'RE INVITED! Bring anyone you can think of. My new friend Jesus is going to be there. I want you to meet Him."

Of course, Jesus showed up. When Jesus approached Matthew at his place of employment, He was genuinely interested in a tax-taker who had no sense of significance in his life. The Nazarene rabbi had His heat sensors on anyone who was hungry for a fresh start at life.

So, when Matthew offered to show his guest of honor his well-appointed pad, Jesus most willingly took the VIP tour. He didn't put Matthew down for having such an over-the-top mansion, but he didn't ooh and aah over it either. Matthew could tell that Jesus was more interested in him than in his home.

And Jesus wasn't the only one who showed up. Matthew's down-and-dirty buddies were there too. They wanted to meet the man responsible for causing Matthew to give up his lucrative occupation. Even though Matthew's profession wasn't the most respectable way to make a living, it provided him with a circle of friends he was able to introduce to Jesus.

In other words, Matthew's past experience was part of what he brought to the table. His friendships, his personality, his confidence in working with money, his ability to mingle with the public—all these aspects of the former tax collector's life were abilities he was now able to use to introduce people to Jesus. In fact, as Matthew grew in his faith, he wrote the first book of the New Testament. It's the one that bears his name. It also bears witness to all Matthew had seen and heard growing up in a Jewish community. Of the four accounts of Jesus' life and ministry, Matthew's Gospel best explains the good news of God's love in a way that Jewish people could understand.

Isn't that fascinating? Not only does God call people

to be part of His plan to change the world, He makes use of what they have to offer. You could probably even make a case for believing that the bents and abilities we are born with were given to us in anticipation of the day we would accept Jesus and start serving Him.

Go ahead and look at what you enjoy doing. Sports? Skateboarding? Writing? Hiking through nature? Spending time with friends? Now look inside at how you relate to others. Are you outgoing? Introverted? Are you the class clown? Are you more studious? All these uniquenesses are God's fingerprints in your life. They point to the special ways He wants to use you. Now it's up to you to accept the fact you've been called to serve Him.

TRIBAL TRAINING

• **Document how you became a disciple of Jesus.** Your testimony may not be as dramatic as some you've heard. But it's your story and it's worth getting down on paper. Don't worry about punctuation or grammar. Just describe what was going on in your life before you decided to take Jesus seriously. Then make note of who influenced you spiritually and why you were open to what they shared. Finally, document how Jesus has impacted your life since. You never know who might want to hear how God's been active in your life.

• **Document what you enjoy doing or are good at.** The way God wired you is part of His calling on your life. You are one of a kind. Write down what people tend to say you're good at. Make note of your achievements, honors, projects you've tackled. Make a list of what you would enjoy doing if you didn't have homework or a job. What are you capable of doing that gives you a sense of pride? In Romans 12:3-8 the apostle Paul reminds us to have an accurate estimation of our abilities.

• **Document those people you've earned the right to share Jesus with.** In your life so far you've had a chance to get to know a lot of people. Some of them are interested in what interests you. Just as Matthew invited his non-Christian friends to meet Jesus, so you have a network of family and friends whom God is interested in reaching through you. That's part of your call.

• **PRAY IT OUT:** *"Lord, help me understand what it means to belong to You."* Thank Jesus that He called you to be part of His team to reach the world. Ask Him for courage to keep from caving in to what others think is important.

TRIBAL MARKS

A KEY POINT I LEARNED TODAY: _____

_____

_____

_____

_____

_____

HOW I WANT TO GROW: _____

_____

_____

_____

_____

_____

MY PRAYER LIST: _____

_____

_____

_____

_____

_____

SURVIVOR SECRETS

>>>**WEEKLY MEMORY VERSE:** *So God created man in his own image, in the image of God he created him; male and female he created them.* —GENESIS 1:27

TRIBAL QUEST

Tap into the power of serving God through the unique abilities He has given to you.

EXPLORE THE WORD: 1 CORINTHIANS 12

TRIBAL TRUTH

The body is a unit, though it is made up of many parts; and though all its parts are many, they form one body. So it is with Christ. . . . But in fact God has arranged the parts in the body, every one of them, just as he wanted them to be. If they were all one part, where would the body be? —1 CORINTHIANS 12:12, 18-19

TRIBAL FACE

Dave Downing—Spiritually Stoked Snowboarder

Everything goes silent when you drop off a hundred-foot cliff. Time slows down, and you feel like you're flying. Oh, and it's better to exhale. Holding your breath makes you tense and then you flap your arms and lose your balance and . . . ouch, you don't want to go there.

That's what pro snowboarder Dave Downing says anyway, and I'm gonna take his word for it.

Dave talks casually about dropping off cliffs like you might discuss popping off a two-foot jump. Watching him in numerous snowboarding videos, it's easy to start thinking those skyscraper-sized cliffs are really no big deal. Don't get me wrong; it's awe inspiring. But the cliffs actually look like a fairly small part of the thousands of sheer mountain feet that Dave flies down, jumping a rock face here, cutting a huge, sweeping arc into fresh powder there, making it all look so smooth and effortless. The guy's got style.

He's also got a whole lot of respect in the snowboarding industry and a solid walk with Christ. "Dave is the perfect example of how a professional rider should interact with his company, promote himself, promote snowboarding, and at the same time help [those] around him achieve their goals," says Rene Hansen, director of Team Marketing for Burton Snowboards. "Dave is basically *the man!*"

That seems to be a consistent sentiment about Dave both inside and out of the snowboarding world. "He's the real deal. Everybody loves him," says Bob Mackenzie, Dave's friend and pastor at North Coast Calvary Chapel in Carlsbad, California. "He loves God and loves people."

Dave also obviously loves snowboarding. And in a sport often known for its darkness, he recognizes that it's the arena where God has placed him to be a light. "I'm trying to be an example through my life and through what I do. It's hard to be a good example in a sport like snowboarding. But I think that's what God wants me to do," Dave says.

"You don't have to party to be a snowboarder. If you love to snowboard and are a Christian, then be that," Dave says. "Don't try to be somebody else. Just because you see snowboarders or skaters acting a certain way doesn't mean that you have to act that way. You don't have to listen to that kind of music. You don't have to do all that negative stuff. You can be yourself. You can be a Christian and a snowboarder at the same time. You can love God and love life."

There's a warmth and graciousness that comes across when talking with Dave. *Transworld Snowboarding* magazine states, "Dave has influenced everyone he's met for the better; as a person and as a snowboarder he's touched them with his familiarity. . . . Dave makes you feel as if he has always been there in this mad world of snowboarding, and been there as a friend."

Rene describes his friend as "a great, down-to-earth, honest, passionate, and real person."

What great descriptions of a follower of Jesus. Fans and industry insiders obviously notice—and respect—a difference in Dave. "Everybody knows [my wife and I] are Christians," he says. "A lot of people are intrigued by it. I think they see me and the way I live my life and think, *He's living a life he believes in.*"

Dave is living proof that you can walk closely with Christ and excel in whatever area He's gifted you, snowboarding included. He stands out on the mountain because of his riding and his faith. You can too.[1]

What about you? What are you into? What are you good at? When God handcrafted you as a unique individual, He included special gifts and skills for you to use as part of His body. Like Dave Downing, you can use your talents to represent Christ to the world around you, as well as to worship Him and encourage fellow believers.

TRIBAL TRAINING

• **Explore your interests.** Ask yourself: *What am I good at? What really gets me going?* Skating, sports, math, music, writing, drawing? It could be anything. Make a list of your skills and accomplishments, and highlight the ones you're most passionate about. Discovering our identity in Christ and who He has made us to be helps uncover His will in our lives.

• **Put it into practice.** Dave Downing didn't become a pro snowboarder overnight. God gives us natural abilities, but we must work to develop them. That can take time. Be patient if you're struggling to find your unique strengths. Try different activities. See what resonates deep inside you. And put in the necessary practice to improve. Most importantly, seek God's guidance and follow Proverbs 3:5-6: "Trust in the LORD with all your heart and lean not on your own understanding; in all your ways acknowledge him, and he will make your paths straight."

- **Step up and serve.** There's a bigger picture than just you. It's great that God gives us joy in practicing the gifts He's given, but it's part of His will for us all to use those gifts to serve others. How? Get creative. What can you create to point to the greatness of God? What can you say to reflect Christ's love to others who share your passion? First Corinthians 12:24-25 says, "But God has combined the members of the body and has given greater honor to the parts that lacked it, so that there should be no division in the body, but that its parts should have equal concern for each other." Because you are a unique creation, you can uniquely reflect and serve the Creator.

- **Worship before the world.** "Therefore, I urge you, brothers, in view of God's mercy, to offer your bodies as living sacrifices, holy and pleasing to God—this is your spiritual act of worship" (Romans 12:1). Whatever your passion, give it your all, and give your all to God. Surrender your skills and ask the Lord how He wants to use them. Stay humble in your triumphs and thankful in your failures. Keeping Christ at the center of your activities and abilities brings glory to Him. Offering Him the best of what you have and do is a natural way to give Him praise.

- **PRAY IT OUT:** *"Lord, take my talents and use them for Your glory."* Thank God for making you just the way you are. Ask Him for guidance in improving and using your gifts and representing Him in all you do.

TRIBAL MARKS

A KEY POINT I LEARNED TODAY:_____

_____

_____

_____

_____

_____

_____

HOW I WANT TO GROW: _____

_____

_____

_____

_____

_____

_____

MY PRAYER LIST:_____

_____

_____

_____

_____

_____

_____

SURVIVOR SECRETS

>>>**WEEKLY MEMORY VERSE:** *So God created man in his own image, in the image of God he created him; male and female he created them.* —**GENESIS 1:27**

TRIBAL QUEST

When God presents you with an assignment that you think is beyond your abilities, don't be quick to turn it down.

EXPLORE THE WORD: JUDGES 6:11-16

TRIBAL TRUTH

I can do everything through him who gives me strength. —**PHILIPPIANS 4:13**

TRIBAL FACE

Gideon—A Reluctant Warrior

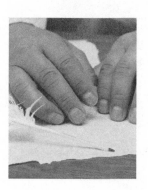

If anyone had an inferiority complex, Gideon did. He was strong and well built, but his physique was dwarfed by his inner fears.

Gideon had grown up in a region of Israel that was routinely ransacked by nomadic warlords from the East. Since surprise attacks were common, people were always on their guard. As a kid Gideon never knew what it was like to play at any distance from home. Even at that, he constantly had to be looking over his shoulder for clouds of dust in the distance that would signal a camel caravan of bloodthirsty Midianites.

As he became a young adult and childhood play gave way to work, Gideon continued to be cautious. Instead of threshing his father's wheat harvest in the open field, he tackled his tasks in a sunken winepress so not to arouse the curiosity of possible looters.

One day an angel of God confronted Gideon and insisted he had no reason to feel insignificant. "God thinks you're a mighty warrior, kid!" Gideon had never thought of "mighty" or "warrior" in relationship to himself. That's not the person he saw looking back at himself in the mirror. He was shy and battled low self-esteem.

The angel went on to say that the Lord was on Israel's side. Gideon balked. "God's on our side? You gotta be kidding. If He's on our side, why do we keep getting our butts kicked by the Midianites?"

Before Gideon could counter the angel's string of ego-boosting statements, he continued. "The Lord has selected you to deliver your family and the rest of Israel from the marauding Midianites."

Gideon slunk back. "You must have the wrong address. I'm no mighty warrior. What's more, there's no way I can deliver my people. My clan's branch of the family tree is the spindliest, and I'm the weakest one of the lot."

In spite of the fact that the leaders of Israel had backed off from their allegiance to Him, the Lord wanted to deliver His people from Midian. He wanted to use Gideon to accomplish His purpose. First things first, though. The altars the leaders of Israel (including Gideon's father) had erected to the pagan gods of Baal and Ashtoreth had to be destroyed.

As a way of demonstrating his allegiance to the One who'd sent an angel to get his attention, Gideon built an altar to the Lord. He was beginning to gain some confidence to break out of his comfort zone. Still he asked the angel to prove that his offering was acceptable. *POOF!* The angel ignited the sacrifice with supernatural fire.

Yet years of squashing his sense of worth had taken its toll. Gideon asked some friends to help him tear down the pagan artifacts in town. But to keep anyone from seeing what they were doing, he insisted they topple them at night while people were asleep.

"If my dad ever finds out, he's really going to be mad!" Gideon told his friends. And he was right. The next day the rubble was discovered, and Gideon was fingered. But amazingly, he didn't get into trouble. The leaders (including Gideon's father) determined that if Baal was upset by what had happened, the god would defend himself.

Maybe God really is going to use me to do great things, Gideon thought to himself, surprised at what he'd gotten away with. Within a matter of days he'd have even more reason to believe God's plans for him were greater than he'd dreamed.

The marauders from the East crossed the Jordan River ready to attack. But the Spirit of the Lord entered Gideon and he found the inner courage to take action. Picking up his rusty trumpet, the would-be warrior blew a long, piercing note that rallied the troops.

As Israel's forces began to gather, Gideon had a momentary lapse of faith. His deep-seated insecurity flared up. He asked the Lord for some kind of proof that he was really the person for this job. He asked for one sign and then another. And both times God answered loud and clear.

With an amazing 32,000 troops at his disposal, Gideon prepared to do battle with the Midianites and their coalition forces.

"Not so fast," the Lord said, calling a time-out. "There are too many Israeli troops. I don't want you to think when this skirmish is over that you pulled this off because of military overload. I want you to realize I'm the One who is giving you the ability to pull off the plans I told you about."

With that, the Lord told Gideon to let all the troops who were battling fear go home. When that option was presented, some 20,000 took off.

Oh my gosh, Gideon thought to himself. *Now I'm the one who's scared. There's no way I can fight the Midianites with such a measly army.*

But even the 10,000 remaining were too many as far as God was concerned. So, He helped His mighty warrior weed out a whole lot more until Gideon was left with only 300. And then against unbelievable odds, the once-insecure Gideon pulled off an amazing victory with fewer soldiers than anyone would have thought possible.

God loves to give people tasks that are way beyond

their ability. He does it on purpose. When they don't rely on their own strength and wisdom, He gets the credit. But that's not all. When God pulls off a victory they weren't capable of, the faith of His warriors grows.

Do you identify with Gideon? Do you struggle with low self-esteem? Does the thought of doing something significant for God leave you weak in the knees? Well, don't be in such a big hurry to disqualify yourself. God may be preparing you to do something really great.

TRIBAL TRAINING

• **Take time to listen to what God wants to do through you.** It's not likely you'll have an angel show up with a message direct from the Lord. But God does have His way of getting our attention. Psalm 32:8 says He takes responsibility for showing us where to go and what to do. Even more, He guides us with His eye on us. The key to figuring out what He's got in mind is to be quiet before Him and consider what He tells us in His Word, through the circumstances around us, and through promptings in our head.

• **Don't be afraid to question God when you doubt what He asks.** It's important to know that God used His man Gideon even though this young guy kept asking God to prove Himself. Hey, the Lord knows we're human and need convincing. When we demonstrate faith it warms His heart, but when we admit we're having a hard time believing what we can't see, His love for us doesn't cool. In the case of Gideon, the Lord met him at the point of his lack of trust and pulled him along.

- **Don't trust in your own ability and dreams.** Our culture values independence and self-sufficiency. Admitting weakness is equated with failure. But in the kingdom of God, admitting you need help is a sign of maturity. Be quick to tell God you feel inadequate. Don't limit your future plans to what you've dreamed up on your own. Be open to opportunities the Lord brings about out of the blue. And remember, God doesn't always call the qualified. More often He qualifies the called . . . after the fact.

- **PRAY IT OUT:** *"Lord, help me be open to Your assignments for which I feel underqualified."* Ask Jesus to clarify His plans for you through the counsel of godly people you trust. Admit your tendency to play it safe instead of stretching your faith muscles.

TRIBAL MARKS

A KEY POINT I LEARNED TODAY:_____

_____

_____

_____

_____

_____

_____

_____

HOW I WANT TO GROW: _____

_____

_____

_____

_____

_____

_____

MY PRAYER LIST:_____

_____

_____

_____

_____

_____

_____

SURVIVOR SECRETS

>>>**WEEKLY MEMORY VERSE:** *So God created man in his own image, in the image of God he created him; male and female he created them.* —**GENESIS 1:27**

TRIBAL QUEST

Shake free from the world's definition of success, which includes money, possessions, and power. Set your vision of accomplishment on loving others and working for the kingdom of heaven.

EXPLORE THE WORD: 1 TIMOTHY 6:3-20

TRIBAL TRUTH

But godliness with contentment is great gain. For we brought nothing into the world, and we can take nothing out of it. —**1 TIMOTHY 6:6-7**

TRIBAL FACE

Rich Mullins—Musician and Servant

Most guys have dreamed of being a rock star. Just think of all that worldwide attention from screaming fans, many of them girls. Imagine the fame of gracing magazine covers, the thrill of flying around the world to play in huge arenas. Imagine the fancy cars and beach homes, the killer home theater and video game systems, the bling of raking in big money. *Well, I'd be a Christian singer, performing for God—but I could still buy some really cool stuff,* you justify.

Now picture this: A successful Christian music artist and his band are just beginning to rehearse. They have a busy tour ahead and lots of preparation left. Their hits are climbing the charts, and they must perfect some new songs before heading out on the road. They have just begun playing the first song when a little girl appears in the doorway. Instead of calling security, sending her away, or making her wait until later, the band's front man stops practice, invites her in, lets her play the keyboard and drums, and spends valuable practice time with her.

Crazy? Maybe. But this scene was common for Rich Mullins. Having visited Native American reservations over the years, his love for the people grew into a deep passion to see their lives transformed. So the artist packed up his life and moved into a trailer on the Navajo Nation reservation in the middle of New Mexico. He spent the last two years of his life there before dying in a car accident in 1997.

The move to the reservation didn't mark the beginning of Rich's love for people more than stuff. It was just an extension of the way he lived his life. Rich's music career was very successful according to the world: numerous No. 1 hits, including "Awesome God" and "Step by Step," which are still being sung in churches. But Rich lived by a different definition of success. He maintained a firm focus on the facts that this life is short and that there is a real eternity yet to come.

Rich believed that the freedom to truly live and love comes from simplicity. He made a considerable amount of money from his music, but he never saw most of it—literally. Early in his career, he asked someone else to handle his money, paying Rich a workingman's salary of approximately $22,000 a year and giving away the rest. He didn't even want to know how much he had. To Rich, it all was God's anyway.

Did he believe you had to be poor to be a truly committed Christian? Hardly. Rich came to the conclusion that God intends for us to have the material things we need, but it's our attitude toward those things that is most important. The right attitude is to have and enjoy what we need, and praise God for it without being captive to it.

In *Rich Mullins: An Arrow Pointing to Heaven,* a devotional biography of Rich's life, author and friend James Bryan Smith wrote, "Instead of storing up treasures on earth, Rich is now enjoying the treasure he stored up in heaven. I've been told that the treasures we store up in heaven are the lives we helped to change, the moments we gave ourselves away for the good of others, and the things we gave away in order to help someone who was in need. If that is true, then Rich Mullins is today a very wealthy man."[1]

Rich gave up his worldly wealth in order to love others. But God still used His resources to fulfill Rich's dreams. Shortly before he died, Rich shared with a friend his vision to provide camps on the reservation for Native American children to learn about music and the gospel. At Rich's death, a foundation funded by the resources he left was established and now provides music camps on the Navajo reservation and around the world. He left a legacy of love by living his life according to a different definition of success.

Are you living for the stuff our culture says is important? Or are you living simply with the freedom to love others sacrificially?

TRIBAL TRAINING

• **Unstuff.** How much energy do you spend wanting and getting more material possessions? How much energy do you spend loving others? "It's a firm conviction that the things of this world are nice but passing, that money and fame cannot buy us happiness, that what we really need and deeply desire is to be in union with God," Rich said.[2]

Do you believe that? Are there any things that are exceptions to this rule in your mind? "But godliness with contentment is great gain. . . . If we have food and clothing, we will be content with that" (1 Timothy 6:6, 8). Make a list. Be honest. Really evaluate how you view material stuff. Ask God to shape your values.

• **Give it away.** "For we brought nothing into the world, and we can take nothing out of it" (1 Timothy 6:7). With that in mind, find something you can get rid of that will bring you more freedom to love others. Start with stuff you don't want or need. Load it up and donate it to a local charity. Then take it to the next level. It's easy to get rid of what you don't want—now get rid of some things you value but know entangle you. Not sure where to start? Try something others need or that you suspect takes your attention away from God.

• **Love like Christ.** How did Christ love others? Sacrificially. Consistently. Unconditionally. First Timothy 6:9-10 warns us that the desire to get rich can cause us to fall into temptation and that the love of money can lead us toward evil. Jesus knew that the things of this world were temporary, so He didn't spend His energy on getting them. Think of one person to whom you would like to show God's love. Think of one selfless way to do that this week. Make a plan and put God's love into action.

• **Forget about it.** "Christianity isn't about being self-sacrificing—it's about being self-forgetting," Rich said.[3] He viewed all people, especially the downtrodden, as his friends. What does it look like to lay down your life? Standing up for someone at school, giving time to serve the homeless, taking the trash out for your mom? Action doesn't have to be super-spiritual to be motivated by love. How can you forget about you and serve those around you?

• **PRAY IT OUT:** *"God, please save me from those things that might distract me. Please take them away and purify my heart. I don't want to lose the eternal for the things that are passing."* Remember Rich Mullins's words: "What will I have when the world is gone, if it isn't for the love that goes on and on with my one thing. You're my one thing."[4]

TRIBAL MARKS

A KEY POINT I LEARNED TODAY:_____

_____

_____

_____

_____

_____

_____

HOW I WANT TO GROW: _____

_____

_____

_____

_____

_____

_____

MY PRAYER LIST:_____

_____

_____

_____

_____

_____

_____

SURVIVOR SECRETS

▶▶▶**WEEKLY MEMORY VERSE:** *So God created man in his own image, in the image of God he created him; male and female he created them.* —**GENESIS 1:27**

TRIBAL QUEST

Set your sights on the ultimate destination, and set some goals to get there.

EXPLORE THE WORD: 2 PETER 3:8-18

TRIBAL TRUTH

But the day of the Lord will come like a thief. The heavens will disappear with a roar; the elements will be destroyed by fire, and the earth and everything in it will be laid bare. Since everything will be destroyed in this way, what kind of people ought you to be? You ought to live holy and godly lives as you look forward to the day of God and speed its coming. —**2 PETER 3:10-12**

TRIBAL FACE

Young Backpacker—Lost
JEREMY V. JONES

We were lost somewhere in the wilderness of Tennessee—or was it North Carolina? It was near the border, so who knows where we were at that exact moment? We sure didn't.

I looked at my compass for the 20th time in as many minutes. "It still says south," I said to my friend David Wilkerson.

David had much more wilderness experience than I did, and he was convinced we should be heading north to reconnect with our trail. Even though this was my first backpacking trip, I knew you were supposed to trust your compass. Mine said we were heading in the exact opposite direction. I was losing what little confidence I had left—and gaining nervousness—quickly.

We'd lost the trail hours earlier. We didn't even realize it at first. It was early spring in the Appalachian Mountains, so early that forest service crews hadn't had a chance to clear the winter's deadfall. We figured that out when we encountered a huge tree blocking the trail.

After climbing around the tangled limbs, we thought we'd found our path again. Granted, it wasn't as well worn as the trail we'd been following, but that could be due to having little use in the winter, we reasoned.

The trail grew fainter the farther we went until we were bushwhacking blindly. It was about this time we decided to consult our map—finally. David thought he had a general idea of where we were. Rather than backtrack and get ourselves more lost, we reasoned, we should head north where eventually we would reconnect with our trail—*if* we were right.

And if we were wrong? David pointed out that we had plenty of food if we had to spend an extra night in the wild. That seemed okay now in the clear, sunny weather, but what if it were like last night? Hiking in we hadn't planned to encounter snow to our knees and ice covering every tree branch in sight. We'd planned to refill our bottles for drinking and cooking in a spring shown on the map, but the snow cover made it impossible to find. We could go without resupplying our water for one night, but hydration would be necessary for survival.

"Look, we can follow this animal path straight down the mountain toward the river and our trail," David said. The uprooted mess of freshly churned dirt, leaves, and debris plunged steeply down the mountainside. It had most likely been created (destroyed was more like it) by wild boars—*ulp!*

My uneasiness turned to flat-out fear. I did not like our circumstances. I loved sleeping under the stars, but I had never been this far away from roads, restaurants, and rescue. We were miles from the car, and we hadn't seen another soul on or anywhere near the trail. Now we didn't even know where that trail was. No doubt about it, we were lost.

It's a wonder I fell in love with backpacking. Eventually, David and I found our trail. Several hours of bushwhacking straight down the mountainside actually cut off a whole day's worth of our original plans for the journey. But, boy, was I happy to reach the car again.

The blunders of that first expedition taught me some valuable lessons. Now I make sure I prepare before heading into the wilderness. I look at maps and make my plan, check the weather and conditions, gather my gear and know how to use it, and find at least one trusted partner. (As for that compass of mine? I finally figured out that it was broken; no matter what direction I faced, the compass said south.)

Although these steps can seem like a hassle when I'm anxious to hit the trail, they pay off in the wild when I have what I need, when I need it to enjoy the experience and the majesty around me. Plus, the more I do it, the more preparation becomes second nature.

I've also realized that similar steps are necessary in our spiritual lives. Our time on earth is a journey, both physically and spiritually. There's a start and an end and plenty of challenges along the way. But God has given us the tools we need to make it. With a little preparation and planning, we can sharpen our spiritual survival skills, build confidence in Christ, and be better equipped to walk His path for our lives.

Are you ready to hit the trail?

TRIBAL TRAINING

• **Know your final destination.** Jesus told us to expect trouble in this world (John 16:33). The Bible tells us that the devil is prowling, looking for a way to destroy us (1 Peter 5:8). Ultimately, we're all going to die unless Christ returns first, but God has prepared a final destination for those who know Him (John 14:2). Understanding the big picture of your life and its ultimate end will guide you along the way. Knowing where you are going will determine what's important along the way and guide your vision past obstacles.

• **Go for goals.** You've got your ultimate destination, but how will you get there? What are the steps along the way? As I found out the hard way, it's not smart to set foot on a trail without being well prepared. "You ought to live holy and godly lives as you look forward to the day of God and speed its coming" (2 Peter 3:11-12). Prayerfully setting goals for spiritual growth (Bible study, prayer, Scripture memorization), service (youth group projects, missions trips), and personal development (hobbies, interests) will allow God to guide you in the right direction and keep you pointed toward eternity when the path seems unclear.

• **Pause to prepare.** Wandering in the wild without a plan will leave you frustrated at best, and suffering or in danger at worst. Wandering spiritually will do the same. It's impossible to anticipate every challenge along the way, but planning ahead can help you be ready to face the challenges when they arise. For example, making a predetermined commitment to sexual purity will steer you clear of trouble before you find yourself in a tempting situation with nothing but the desire of the moment to fall back on.

• **Take the right tools.** You must also have the right gear—and know how to use it. Merely throwing a cheap compass in your pack isn't any help if you don't know how to use it or if it's unreliable. And having the latest, greatest, warmest down parka won't do any good in 90-degree weather. At the same time, having the biggest, coolest teen study Bible won't help you at all sitting on your shelf.

■ **Don't walk alone.** It's a good thing I wasn't on the trail alone. I might not have made it back alive. Deciding who—and what—you take on the trail with you are also important preparations. A good backpacking partner has solid wilderness skills and can help you bear your burden. He is someone you can count on in a jam who will encourage you to keep going and sharpen your own skills. A solid Christian brother can share your struggles and give you a hand when you're down.

Who can you count on and learn from on the spiritual trail?

■ **PRAY IT OUT:** *"Father, direct my paths in light of Your overall purpose for my life."* Thank God for His ultimate plan for eternity. Ask Him to direct you in setting and accomplishing goals that bring Him glory. Ask Him to shape your character on life's journey.

TRIBAL MARKS

A KEY POINT I LEARNED TODAY:_____

_____

_____

_____

_____

_____

_____

HOW I WANT TO GROW: _____

_____

_____

_____

_____

_____

_____

MY PRAYER LIST:_____

_____

_____

_____

_____

_____

_____

A WARRIOR'S CALLING

KNOW WHAT YOU BELIEVE
WEEK 2

SURVIVOR SECRETS

You alone are the Lord. You made the heavens, even the highest heavens, and all their starry host, the earth and all that is on it, the seas and all that is in them. You give life to everything, and the multitudes of heaven worship you. —**NEHEMIAH 9:6**

TRIBAL QUEST

Revolutionize your relationship with the heavenly Father by grasping His love for you.

EXPLORE THE WORD: JAMES 1:17-18

TRIBAL TRUTH

Every good and perfect gift is from above, coming down from the Father of the heavenly lights, who does not change like shifting shadows. —**JAMES 1:17**

TRIBAL FACE

C. S. Lewis—Thinker and Apologist

You've probably heard of C. S. Lewis, perhaps the greatest articulator of Christian faith in the twentieth century and author of the popular "Chronicles of Narnia" books. But were you aware that Lewis was for years an avowed atheist, denying the very existence of God and wanting nothing to do with Christianity? Jack, as he was called by friends, may have remained that way were it not for the persistent love of a heavenly Father calling and pulling this lost son to come back to Himself.

Though raised in a happy Christian home, Lewis's world blew apart at age nine when his mother died. Hardly able to deal with the loss of his wife, Jack's father, Albert Lewis, sent his son to boarding school. It felt like banishment to the young grieving boy, and he planted seeds of anger toward his father that would eventually grow into a strong bitterness. Perhaps that same sense of pain was what started the boy Jack on a path away from God.

As Lewis continued his education and studied under secular teachers, he grew more and more disdainful of God. At age 17, he explained bluntly to longtime friend Arthur Greeves: "I believe in no religion. There is absolutely no proof for any of them, and from a philosophical standpoint Christianity is not even the best."[1]

He later confessed that he viewed God as the "great interferer."[2] Lewis planned to be an accomplished poet and wanted to walk through life on his own terms. As he advanced within the academic world, Lewis was on a constant quest to defy God and disprove his need for any higher authority. But God had other plans.

"Really, a young Atheist cannot guard his faith too carefully," Lewis wrote later in life. "Danger lies in wait for him on every side."[3]

You might say that C. S. Lewis came to faith in two distinct conversions. His first step was from atheism into the acceptance that there was indeed a God.

"In the Trinity Term of 1929 I gave in, and admitted that God was God, and knelt and prayed: perhaps, that night, the most dejected and reluctant convert in all England."[4]

He gave in grudgingly, but at that point was missing an important realization about his heavenly Father. "I did not then see what is now the most shining and obvious thing; the Divine humility which will accept a convert even on such terms. The Prodigal Son at least walked home on his own feet. But who can duly adore the Love which will open the high gates to a prodigal who is brought in kicking, struggling, resentful, and darting his eyes in every direction for a chance of escape?"[5]

To put it in more earthly terms, it was as if Lewis were handed the keys to a brand-new Ferrari and said, "Okay, fine. If I must drive this super sports car, I'll do it, but I'm not happy about it."

Two years later after listening to influential friends including J. R. R. Tolkien, Jack took the final step, believing in and surrendering his life to Christ. "I have just passed on from believing in God to definitely believing in Christ," he wrote to his friend Arthur Greeves.[6]

Lewis had finally gained a full realization of God's compassionate love as a Father and returned home. If he had been a reluctant prodigal earlier, now he understood the magnitude of God's love demonstrated in sacrificing His own Son Jesus.

What a gracious God to keep His arms wide open and welcome a man so set against Him for so long! But like an encouraging father who sees the greatest potential in

his child, God urged C. S. Lewis along in his spirit, drawing Lewis to Himself even while the man rebelled against His unconditional love.

The Creator had formed C. S. Lewis with an incredible mind and ability to communicate. Once Lewis surrendered his life, his heavenly Father was able to use the man as a mighty mouthpiece. Even decades after Lewis's death, his writings continue to challenge readers and declare God's glory around the world.

How is your relationship with your heavenly Father? Do you realize the magnitude of the fact that the Creator of the universe longs for you? Or are you a spiritual rebel, running from the One who loves you most?

TRIBAL TRAINING

• **Who's your daddy?** There's no avoiding it. How you view your relationship with your earthly father affects how you view your heavenly Father. So how are things with Dad? List at least three ways you can improve interaction. Maybe it's spending time together on a shared hobby or asking his advice with a problem. Be creative.

• **Get good gifts.** Sometimes it feels like your parents are always the bad cops. But believe it or not, they're thrilled deep down inside to make you happy. Jesus said, "If you, then, though you are evil, know how to give good gifts to your children, how much more will your Father in heaven give good gifts to those who ask him!" (Matthew 7:11). God's love for you is indescribable. Open your heart and ask Him to help you experience it.

- **Don't dodge discipline.** Often our own sin and disobedience throw obstacles between us and the Father. He has to discipline us to remove those barriers. Though our conscience can make us feel guilty, God is always ready to cleanse and restore us. It's Satan who heaps on the condemnation. Keep God's perspective in mind: "Endure hardship as discipline; God is treating you as sons. . . . Our fathers disciplined us for a little while as they thought best; but God disciplines us for our good, that we may share in his holiness. No discipline seems pleasant at the time, but painful. Later on, however, it produces a harvest of righteousness and peace for those who have been trained by it" (Hebrews 12:7, 10-11).

- **Come running.** Read the story of the prodigal son (Luke 15:11-32). What an amazing picture of God as our Father! And what an example of God's patient pursuit is C. S. Lewis's life. Are you resisting God's fatherly love? What are you wallowing in instead? Get up, shake off your sin, and lay it at God's feet. He can't wait to throw His arms around you and celebrate you as His precious son. It's time to join His party.

- **PRAY IT OUT:** *"Father, thank You for Your amazing love."* Ask God to let you feel His love like never before. Ask for His discipline to spark your spiritual life, and pray that He will repair your relationship with your earthly dad.

TRIBAL MARKS

A KEY POINT I LEARNED TODAY: _____

_____

_____

_____

_____

_____

_____

HOW I WANT TO GROW: _____

_____

_____

_____

_____

_____

_____

MY PRAYER LIST: _____

_____

_____

_____

_____

_____

_____

SURVIVOR SECRETS

>>>WEEKLY MEMORY VERSE: *You alone are the LORD. You made the heavens, even the highest heavens, and all their starry host, the earth and all that is on it, the seas and all that is in them. You give life to everything, and the multitudes of heaven worship you.* —NEHEMIAH 9:6

TRIBAL QUEST

When you're guilty of failing God, admit you're wrong and claim His forgiveness.

EXPLORE THE WORD: MARK 14:27-31, 66-72

TRIBAL TRUTH

No temptation has seized you except what is common to man. And God is faithful; he will not let you be tempted beyond what you can bear. But when you are tempted, he will also provide a way out so that you can stand up under it. —1 CORINTHIANS 10:13

TRIBAL FACE

Peter—A Curious Case of Denial

Pete was looking forward to graduation. He'd just completed a three-year graduate program focusing on advanced fisheries. Compared to the small-potatoes fishing operation his dad and brothers ran, this new approach to the industry was in a category all by itself. Peter's exposure to his field education had pretty much determined he would not be going back to work his father's boats. There was just no comparison. The bait was different and the results were out of this world.

The three-year program had gone fast. He and the other members of his class credited their mentor with that. Joshua was a remarkable teacher. Josh, as the grad students called him, had been a master woodworker before making his mark in the "fisheries" field. His style of teaching was very hands-on and student-centered. Rather than following the traditional pattern of classroom instruction, Josh was big on lab experiences and outdoor training. Even though their teacher hadn't directly said so, the dozen or so in the program felt they were involved in watershed research that would result in writing the bible of high-tech fishing.

But as much as Pete was anticipating finishing his coursework, he was troubled. It was something Josh had said last night at a formal dinner in which the graduating class was recognized. Cornering Pete after the meal, Josh said, "I have a funny feeling you are about to discredit our research and trash my reputation here at the university. And I want you to know I'm troubled by it."

Pete was totally caught off guard by Josh's words. "I resent that!" he said in self-defense. "There is no way in the world I would ever do such a thing. I respect you, Josh. I'm proud of what we've accomplished together."

Josh, somewhat out of character, wouldn't let it drop. "Believe me, Pete, I know what I'm talking about even if you don't. Don't make it worse by being so defensive."

Pete's face reddened with anger as he insisted on his innocence. "The rest of our class may be capable of doing what you're accusing me of, but not me. I'm as loyal as they come."

As Pete replayed the conversation from last night in his head, he felt some remorse from losing his cool. He felt worse, however, over what his mentor had said. Because he had so much respect for Josh, it was difficult for him to make sense of the fact that Josh couldn't see that.

About this time the phone rang. It was James from down the hall. "Did you see the police car pull up in front of the dorm? They just took Josh away in handcuffs. My brother John said he'd overheard someone say something about fraud."

Pete slammed down the phone and ran down the two flights of stairs to the entrance to the dormitory. All the while he was trying to piece together this strange set of circumstances. *How could Josh be guilty of fraud?* he asked himself. *The guy is as honest as they come.*

When he got to the lobby, he could see the squad car pulling away. There was no need for a siren, but the light bar on top of the sedan was flashing. Pete started to head back up to his room when he saw a news reporter and a camera crew from the local television station setting up their remote equipment. He leaned against the Coke machine to try and hear what the reporter would say. Just then, a technician with earphones on walked by.

"Are you a student in the fisheries program?" he asked. "Do you know Joshua Josephson?"

The question caught him by surprise. He amazed him-self by not answering right away. Instead he just stood there feeling flush. "Didn't you hear me?" the tech con-tinued, sounding a bit perturbed. "Do you know Dr. Josephson or not?"

Pete's thoughts were fast-forwarding in his head. This was the TV station that fed its signal by satellite to 50 cities around the country (including the coastal city where his folks lived). If he admitted to knowing Josh, would they interview him on the evening news? If they did, would his family and friends back home think he was tied to Josh's alleged guilt?

"Never heard of the guy!" Pete finally managed to reply. The technician accepted his denial and proceeded to set up some equipment. But Pete froze in place. It dawned on him his name could be easily traced on the class roster and his deception would be exposed.

Wanting to cover his tracks he walked up to the tech and said, "Wait, what did you say his name was? Josephson? Oh yeah, I thought you said some other name. I know him. He's a real jerk. Some people think he fudged some of the facts on his résumé."

As the technician waved for the reporter to talk to Pete, a dog outside the front entrance barked. Pete was dying inside. He knew he was in the doghouse.

You know this story, right? The Hebrew name for Jesus is Joshua. It was that Joshua, son of Joseph, who left His father's carpentry profession to teach a dozen willing wanna-bes a new kind of fishing. Peter was a commercial fisherman who was one of Jesus' most ardent students of fishing for people. But in spite of his enthusiasm, Peter failed his Lord by bailing on Him.

In Peter we see ample evidence that in a fallen world, good and decent people aren't perfect. They are flawed and prone to sinful choices. Peter isn't the only one tempted to deny he's a follower of Jesus because of what his friends might think. We all find ourselves in that kind of situation from time to time. Fortunately, Peter wasn't in the doghouse very long. After Jesus died and came back to life, He forgave Peter for being a chicken when the rooster crowed.

Are you aware of just how prone you are to fail the Lord? It's easy to come off sounding more committed than you really are. But you're spiritually challenged just like the next guy, and believe it or not, the sooner you recognize your vulnerability to fail, the stronger you'll become.

TRIBAL TRAINING

• **Don't dismiss your spiritual weakness out of hand.** Even though it's humbling to admit your tendency to sin, you know deep down how weak you are. So does Jesus. But He loves you just the same. Since we can't fool the Lord and since He isn't going to quit loving us when we blow it, we need to recognize our flawed nature.

• **Make note of your signature sin.** Everybody has

one temptation that tends to trip him up more than another. Hebrews 12:1-3 refers to this as the sin that "so easily entangles." It might be a pull toward a sin that will fade over time. Or it may be a temptation you might need to fight all your life. It could be lust, deceit, laziness, or even anger. But if you admit your vulnerability and ask the Lord to help you deal with it, you will make more progress than if you don't.

• **Keep short accounts with God.** Being a Christian doesn't mean you don't sin anymore. In fact, you may be more aware of sin in your life than ever before. The key is to admit your sin to God and ask Him to cleanse you of it.

• **PRAY IT OUT:** *"Lord, help me to keep short accounts with You."* Admit to Jesus just how vulnerable you are to sin. Confess to Him what you've said, thought about, or done today that you are sorry for.

TRIBAL MARKS

A KEY POINT I LEARNED TODAY:_____

_____

_____

_____

_____

_____

_____

HOW I WANT TO GROW: _____

_____

_____

_____

_____

_____

_____

MY PRAYER LIST:_____

_____

_____

_____

_____

_____

_____

SURVIVOR SECRETS

>>>**WEEKLY MEMORY VERSE**: *You alone are the LORD. You made the heavens, even the highest heavens, and all their starry host, the earth and all that is on it, the seas and all that is in them. You give life to everything, and the multitudes of heaven worship you.* —**NEHEMIAH 9:6**

TRIBAL QUEST

Trust that the members of the Godhead are equal in power and glory and cooperate in the work of creation, salvation, and sanctification. We believe this, not because we understand it, but because the Bible teaches it and the Holy Spirit testifies in our hearts to this truth.

EXPLORE THE WORD: MATTHEW 3:1-17

TRIBAL TRUTH

As soon as Jesus was baptized, he went up out of the water. At that moment heaven was opened, and he saw the Spirit of God descending like a dove and lighting on him. And a voice from heaven said, "This is my Son, whom I love; with him I am well pleased." —**MATTHEW 3:16-17**

TRIBAL FACE

John the Baptist—Trusting the Trinity

John the Baptist couldn't believe what his cousin had just asked. Jesus—the One who claimed to be the

Messiah, the Son of God, the Lord of all creation—wanted to be baptized and insisted that John was the one to do it.

"I need to be baptized by You, and do You come to *me?*" John asked.

Yet Jesus was serious: "Let it be so now; it is proper for us to do this to fulfill all righteousness."

Jesus knew that He didn't need to be cleansed, but He pointed out that He needed to identify fully with the people to whom He was sent. What's more, His Father had chosen this occasion to publicly declare that Jesus is the Son of God and is empowered by the Spirit of God.

It was a moment that changed humanity forever. Heaven opened, and the Spirit of God descended on Jesus like a dove. It was also the first time since Creation that God publicly revealed His amazing nature: There are three Persons who relate to each other as Father (the voice), Son (Jesus), and Holy Spirit (in the form of a dove); yet there is only One of Him.

"This is My Son, whom I love," announced a voice from heaven. "With Him I am well pleased."

John probably had many questions after this intense experience. *Could Jesus really be the Son and Savior who is foretold in the Old Testament? Is He really God on earth? And what about that bird; what did it mean?*

The mystery of the Trinity has stirred debate among mankind for centuries—probably because of our limited capacity to comprehend it. Yet one way of understanding this mystery is by looking at man himself.

A man can be a son (to his parents), a father (to his children), and a husband (to his wife). He is all three things at once, and still he's one person. In the same way, we have one God, but He's three Persons.

Perhaps a better illustration of the Trinity is that of *light, heat,* and *air.* Author and scholar James Montgomery Boice explains it this way in his book *The Sovereign God:* "If you hold out your hand and look at it, each of these three things is present. There is light, because it is only by light that you can see your hand. . . . There is also heat between your head and your hand. You can prove it by holding out a thermometer. It will vary as you go from a cold room to a warm room or from the outside to indoors. Finally, there is air. You can blow on your hand and feel it. You can wave your hand and thus fan your face."[1]

Boice points out that while *light, heat,* and *air* are distinct from each other, it is impossible to have any one without the others (at least in an earthly setting). They are three and yet they are one.

The Bible speaks of each of these elements in rela-tion to God—light (1 John 1:5), heat (Hebrews 12:29), air (John 3:8). Scripture also makes clear that Jesus Christ is fully divine, being the second Person of the Godhead who became man: "The Word became flesh and made his dwelling among us. We have seen his glory, the glory of the One and Only, who came from the Father, full of grace and truth" (John 1:14).

• **Take comfort:** Salvation as a whole is attributed to the Trinity. Check out 1 Peter 1:2, which says that we are "chosen according to the foreknowledge of God the Father, through the sanctifying work of the Spirit, for obedience to Jesus Christ and sprinkling by his blood."

• **Recognize the strategy of the enemy.** The Christmas story may seem Sunday-school sweet, but what lies behind the stable is a brutal battle. Satan's determination to dominate the sons of Adam and the daughters of Eve is ruthless. It's a bloody war. Be on your guard for one who prowls like a roaring lion seeking to devour you (1 Peter 5:8). Remember that Jesus is alive. One of the names for Jesus is Immanuel. That means "God is with us." That's in the present tense. He continues to be with us and for us. In Him you have the power to stand up to Satan's lies and deceptive traps.

• **PRAY IT OUT:** *"Lord, I will forever be grateful that You entered into our world to be able to understand the issues I face."* Tell Jesus what some of the temptations you are currently dealing with are. Ask Him to stand with you against Satan.

TRIBAL MARKS

A KEY POINT I LEARNED TODAY: _____

_____

_____

_____

_____

_____

_____

HOW I WANT TO GROW: _____

_____

_____

_____

_____

_____

_____

MY PRAYER LIST: _____

_____

_____

_____

_____

_____

_____

SURVIVOR SECRETS

▶▶▶**WEEKLY MEMORY VERSE:** *You alone are the LORD. You made the heavens, even the highest heavens, and all their starry host, the earth and all that is on it, the seas and all that is in them. You give life to everything, and the multitudes of heaven worship you.* **—NEHEMIAH 9:6**

TRIBAL QUEST

When you feel like no one cares about you, just think about what Jesus did on the cross and afterward to guarantee you'll spend eternity with Him.

EXPLORE THE WORD: MATTHEW 27:27–28:11

TRIBAL TRUTH

But he was pierced for our transgressions, he was crushed for our iniquities; the punishment that brought us peace was upon him, and by his wounds we are healed. **—ISAIAH 53:5**

TRIBAL FACE

The Passion of the Christ

It was the same cobblestone road. But it was an entirely different scene.

On Sunday, Jesus was the welcomed burden on a willing burro. He paraded into Jerusalem to the sound of joyful shouts as crowds of people praised Him. Now it was Friday. Five short days had changed the script and the plot.

Today, rather than riding an animal, Jesus was being treated as if he were an animal. Today He Himself was the beast of burden. And the load He was forced to carry was a heavy Roman cross. The shouts of the crowd were not happy ones. Instead of "Hosanna!" they cried "Crucify Him!" The 33-year-old Carpenter-Turned-Rabbi stumbled forward under the weight of the cedar beam.

Jesus' lack of strength was not really due to the fact that he'd been up all night. While that was true, what had sapped His energy was the way He'd spent the hours since midnight. Soldiers had spit on Him. They pummeled Him with their angry fists. They flogged Him with whips tipped with glass, bone, and metal. They even created a makeshift crown that raked His skin to the point of bloodshed when they crushed it down on His head.

Jesus knew His purpose in coming to earth could not be accomplished without unimaginable suffering and tor-ture. He also knew that He was the only one who could break the spell that had been cast on the world ever since Adam and Eve were kicked out of Eden.

Because Jesus kept falling as He tried to shoulder the cross, a stranger, chosen at random by the guards, was forced to carry it for Him. At first the surrogate cross-bearer was red-faced with anger. An out-of-the-blue com-mand had interrupted his busy day preparing for the Passover. Jesus' blood that had drenched the cross was now on him. The crowds jeered him as if he were the condemned man. But Jesus was stumbling behind him. Finally at the top of a hill, the soldiers told the man to drop the cross. As he did, his eyes met Jesus' eyes.

The warm brown eyes of the wounded healer made the stranger feel warm all over. He felt loved. He felt accepted. His whole attitude about being forced to carry the cross changed. For some crazy reason he felt like he had been given a special honor.

But before the man could think any more about it, he was shoved aside by a Roman centurion and forced to watch from the sidelines.

"Hold the rabbi still," the centurion shouted at the two soldiers who pinned Jesus to the crossbeams while a third pounded six-inch spikes into His wrists and ankles. Jesus let out a bloodcurdling scream as the cold metal spikes penetrated His fevered flesh and entered the wood on which He was stretched. And then when the cross was lifted and dropped into a waiting hole in the ground, He shrieked in pain.

For the next three hours thick, black storm clouds crowded overhead. A steady rain fell. Jarring claps of thunder and jagged beams of lightning added a sound-and-light show to the public execution.

As Jesus hung on the cross bleeding profusely, He pushed up with His feet in order to breathe. Physically He was in agony. But His torture was not limited to what was going on in His body as it slowly shut down. The real suffering Jesus experienced was something nobody standing around the cross knew anything about.

The perfect Son of God who had willingly left heaven to experience life on an imperfect planet was becoming the ultimate scapegoat. The only innocent one to ever live was taking on Himself all the sin of all the people who had ever lived or would ever live.

There's no way of beginning to imagine what it was

like. Oh sure, you know what guilt feels like. But try multiplying that feeling of shame to the billionth power. That's what caused Jesus to suffer. Believe it or not, it was worse than being beaten to within an inch of His life, then forced to carry the cross and finally hammered to it. Much worse.

No wonder He cried, "My God, my God, why have you forsaken me?"[1] Our sins were piled so high and heavy that Jesus couldn't sense His Father anywhere. While His blood poured down to the ground, Jesus looked up and gave up. In a split second, He was motionless. He was dead.

Just then an earthquake shook the ground as most ran for cover. One brave man named Joseph of Arimathea stayed near the bloody cross as the soldiers pulled it up and laid it flat. As they removed Jesus' limp body from it, Joseph wrapped the corpse in strips of white fabric like a mummy. Then he found a couple of friends to help him carry it to a nearby grave.

The black sky gradually became lighter, but the hearts of those who had followed Jesus remained dark. *Was Jesus' promise to be the Savior of the world just talk?* They also feared for their lives. *Will the Romans come looking for us as well?*

Three days later when some friends of Jesus went to pay their respects at His grave, they were in for the shock of their lives. The body wasn't in the tomb. And before they could try and piece together a possible scenario of where it had been taken, two angels appeared and said, "He has risen! He is not here."[2]

Yes, you've heard that story before. But has it really hit you, what took place when Jesus died? Do you understand that the empty tomb means He accomplished what He set out to do on the cross? Have you ever really stopped and thought about the fact that He did it all for you?

TRIBAL TRAINING

• **Remember the cost of your salvation.** You may have seen Mel Gibson's movie *The Passion of the Christ* or another movie version of Jesus' life. If your parents say okay, go ahead and rent a DVD about the Crucifixion and watch it. As you look at the reenactment of what Jesus did for you, let His suffering and pain grip your gut. Tell yourself, *This really happened. And because it did, I don't have to live with guilt. In fact, because it happened, I get to live forever with Jesus.*

• **Let Jesus' death impact your life.** If you believe that Jesus died as punishment for your sin, you will have eternal life. But God desires to give you more than a free ticket to heaven when you die. He wants you to show your gratitude for the Cross by denying your selfish desires and taking up the cross of obedience.

• **Make sure you are forgiven.** If you've never asked Jesus to come into your heart, why not do it today? Thank Him for dying for you and tell Him you want to live for Him.

• **PRAY IT OUT:** *"Lord, thank You for dying on the cross for me."* Tell Jesus you are sorry that your sins are part of the reason He had to suffer so much. Ask Him to forgive you of the sins that you still commit.

TRIBAL MARKS

A KEY POINT I LEARNED TODAY:_____

_____

_____

_____

_____

_____

_____

HOW I WANT TO GROW: _____

_____

_____

_____

_____

_____

_____

MY PRAYER LIST:_____

_____

_____

_____

_____

_____

_____

SURVIVOR SECRETS

▶▶▶**WEEKLY MEMORY VERSE:** *You alone are the Lᴏʀᴅ. You made the heavens, even the highest heavens, and all their starry host, the earth and all that is on it, the seas and all that is in them. You give life to everything, and the multitudes of heaven worship you.* —**Nᴇʜᴇᴍɪᴀʜ 9:6**

TRIBAL QUEST

When you're tempted to dismiss the devil as a figment of your pastor's imagination, think again. He's very real!
EXPLORE THE WORD: Eᴘʜᴇꜱɪᴀɴꜱ 6:10-12

TRIBAL TRUTH

Finally, be strong in the Lord and in his mighty power. Put on the full armor of God so that you can take your stand against the devil's schemes. —**Eᴘʜᴇꜱɪᴀɴꜱ 6:10**

TRIBAL FACE

Christ Overcomes the Enemy

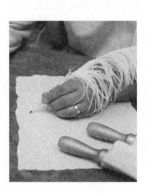

Filled with the Holy Spirit, Jesus journeys deep into the wilderness for some intense "combat training." (See Matthew 4:1-11.) The Savior spends 40 days and nights trekking through the wastelands of Judea—alone, with no food or shelter. It's a savage, desolate terrain, a dangerous place. At night, the temperatures drop to bone-chilling digits. By midday the heat of the sun grows intolerable.

Weary and fighting the dull ache of starvation, Jesus begins the Test.

All at once, a cold presence completely engulfs Jesus. The Lord is suddenly transported to the highest corner of the temple wall. Scattered like pebbles below Him is the Holy City, Jerusalem. Here the priests blow trumpets to usher in the New Year. Here the air is thin and the height is giddy.[1]

The icy light comes into focus and speaks: "Jump," the Deceiver says, "and prove You are the Son of God." The evil presence goads Him, quoting Psalm 91: "For the Scriptures declare, 'God will send His angels to keep You from harm'—they will prevent You from smashing on the rocks below."[2]

Jesus counters with a citation from Deuteronomy: "It also says not to put the Lord your God to a foolish test!"

In a flash, the Holy City vanishes, and Jesus is no longer on the temple wall. He is now infinitely higher than anything made by human hands. Standing on a cosmic mountain, the presence gestures expansively—pointing out all the Earth's kingdoms, how glorious they all are. Then he says, "They're Yours—lock, stock, and barrel. Just fall down on Your knees and worship me, and they're Yours."[3]

But Jesus does not look at the kingdoms of the world, and His refusal is stern: "I know you. I know what sort of angel you are. Satan, tempter, betrayer—get out of here!" The Savior backs His rebuke with another quotation from Deuteronomy: "Worship the Lord your God, and only Him. Serve Him with absolute single-heartedness."

In an instant, Jesus is sitting in the desert again, leaning against a boulder. The Test is over and the Devil is gone. In place of the icy presence are warmth and peace and goodness. Angels come down from heaven to care for the Savior.

The devil used all his strength and cunning to get Jesus to stumble. But Christ didn't budge. Our Lord and Savior passed the Test and defeated the Enemy.

Yet today, Satan and his evil troops have set their focus on you. The Deceiver knows just which buttons to push to tempt you away from depending on God. He has watched your behavior over the years and knows where you are weak. That's where he attacks.

Satan's very name means *accuser,* and despite what some may think, the Scriptures do not portray him as a mere metaphor or symbol of evil. Satan is a created being who rebelled against God. He is very real, very dangerous, and is at work in the world today, enticing his victims toward evil.

The Bible refers to Satan as "the deceiver" (Revelation 12:9), "an inciter" (1 Chronicles 21:1), "an accuser" (Zechariah 3:1), "a sinner" (1 John 3:8), "a murderer and a liar" (John 8:44). Scriptures make it clear that he is rotten to the core. Satan and his troops are viciously attacking the kingdom of God. His target: our souls.

Despite the reality of his existence, is he as all-powerful as he wants us to believe? Do we have the strength to out-muscle his deadly schemes?

In Job 1:12 we uncover some clues about Satan's limited power: "The LORD said to Satan, 'Very well, then, everything he has is in your hands, but on the man him-self do not lay a finger.' Then Satan went out from the presence of the Lord." In other words, the devil operates on a leash that God holds.

Hebrews 2:14 assures us that the fear Satan held over humanity was rendered powerless by Christ: "Since the children have flesh and blood, he too shared in their humanity so that by his death he might destroy him who holds the power of death—that is, the devil."

As a created being, Satan is not a sovereign, all-powerful being, and he is certainly not equal to God. In the book *Essentials of Spiritual Warfare,* author A. Scott Moreau points out that Christianity is not a dualistic reli-gion, a faith in which two opposing but equal powers struggle for control. "Even so, many Christians live as though Satan were as powerful as God," he writes. "Nothing could be further from the truth! . . . Because God is sovereign Satan does not stand a chance."[4]

Tribal Training

• **Turn to Jesus Christ for the power to with-stand the enemy.** Jesus understands the struggle, and He delivers His children from evil. But know this: Merely hang-ing out at church and "doing your Christian duty" don't cut it. You need to know Jesus personally. He is the greatest conqueror ever, and with His guidance, you can have victo-ry against the devil.

• **Don't be misled.** Are you being deceived? Are you among those who believe that spiritual warfare is pure fantasy—the stuff of chilling novels and thriller movies? The Bible is clear that the Enemy of our souls is very real.

He's ruthless. But he's also deceptive. He appears like an angel of light. Jesus called him the father of lies (John 8:44). He wins when you believe he's only a figment of someone's imagination.

- **Make sure you've got your armor on.** The best way you can be protected from Satan's frontline assault is to be clothed in Christ. Are you really a Christian? Have you personally asked Jesus to take control of your life? If so, you belong to Him and don't have to fear being taken as a spiritual hostage. But to make sure your mind and heart aren't under constant attack from Satan's deceptions and enticing temptations, you need to put on your spiritual armor every day (Ephesians 6:10-12).

- **Have a daily quiet time.** The best way to be suited up in spiritual armor is to connect with Jesus every day. The Lord speaks to us when we read His Word. When we talk to Him in prayer we are more aware of His presence with us. So don't let anything keep you from that time. Also, make sure the place you have chosen will be free from distractions.

- **Establish an accountability relationship.** When you feel like Satan has wrestled you to the mat, whom can you talk to? When you feel like you've been in the presence of darkness and evil, you need to talk about it with someone you trust. Talking to Jesus is important. But it helps to have a friend you can open up to who will also pray with you.

- **PRAY IT OUT:** *"Lord, please protect me from Satan and his clever schemes."* Ask Jesus to prompt you to spend time with Him on a regular basis. Ask Him to make you sensitive to evil situations so you can run from them.

TRIBAL MARKS

A KEY POINT I LEARNED TODAY:_____

_____

_____

_____

_____

_____

_____

HOW I WANT TO GROW: _____

_____

_____

_____

_____

_____

_____

MY PRAYER LIST:_____

_____

_____

_____

_____

_____

SURVIVOR SECRETS

▶▶▶**WEEKLY MEMORY VERSE:** *You alone are the LORD. You made the heavens, even the highest heavens, and all their starry host, the earth and all that is on it, the seas and all that is in them. You give life to everything, and the multitudes of heaven worship you.* —NEHEMIAH 9:6

TRIBAL QUEST

Clip in to your lifeline, God's Word, and encounter a deeper faith in God.

EXPLORE THE WORD: 2 TIMOTHY 3:10-17

TRIBAL TRUTH

All Scripture is God-breathed and is useful for teaching, rebuking, correcting and training in righteousness, so that the man of God may be thoroughly equipped for every good work. —2 TIMOTHY 3:16-17

TRIBAL FACE

Trey Lowman—*Breakaway* Rock Climber

I don't think I can do this!

The words didn't come out of 13-year-old Trey Lowman's mouth, but his mind was chattering nervously and everything about his body language screamed uncertainty—with good reason.

He was distracted by the 60-foot rock face behind him as instructors explained how to put on a harness and clip into a carabiner, his only links to safety six stories above the ground. The face, dubbed Bob's Rock, sounded innocent enough, but its vertical look was another story. Trey had never climbed a cliff before; he wasn't sure he wanted to.

But the instructors were encouraging, the other guys were going for it, and even Trey's dad was going to give it a try. Trey stepped up to the rock, took a deep breath, and began to climb. His hands and feet found crevices and cracks to cling to, and when they had trouble, his dad on the ground guided him to new holds. Before anyone could say Spider-Man, Trey was at the top taking in the spectacular view of the Rocky Mountains, experiencing the adrenaline rush of new heights and success.

Like many things in life, that rock climb looked impossible to Trey from the ground. It was steep and foreboding; he had never before faced anything quite like it. But with some instruction and support, he stepped out in faith.

It's a good thing he had that rope. "Trust the rope," his instructors had said. Anchored securely above, the thin nylon line was strong enough to hold a truck.

Trey wouldn't have tried any of those climbs without the safety of good equipment. To do otherwise would be suicide. No matter how much balance and strength a climber possesses, there will come a time when he slips and falls. "Even youths grow tired and weary, and young men stumble and fall," Isaiah 40:30 says. That's when good rope is vital. It prevents disaster when anchored solidly and hooked to a trusted belay buddy (the person responsible for holding the rope and taking up the slack as the climber heads up the rock). Even when the climber slips, a properly used rope will keep the fall short, controlled, and safe.

Once on the rock, Trey's supporters on the ground quickly faded from view until he couldn't see them, but their shouts continued to encourage him. As you head up the rock face of most climbs, your belayer becomes invisible pretty quickly. Outcroppings and cracks block your view of the person in whose hands you have placed your life. It's similar to trusting an invisible God in our everyday lives.

Thankfully, God has provided His Word as a direct link to Him. In many ways, the Bible is like a climbing rope; it is your lifeline. It guides you in the direction you should go. It catches you when you fall. Its presence gives comfort and confidence. It keeps you connected to God Himself, your ultimate belayer and sustainer. It preserves your life.

Are you tied into God's Word as your lifeline, or are you free-climbing dangerously through life, flirting with a deadly fall? Do you believe that God's Word is strong enough to instruct and sustain you? Are you relying on it daily?

• **Tie into your lifeline.** A rope lying unused at the bottom of a cliff does no good. Neither does a Bible collecting dust on the shelf. Commit now to make Scripture reading a daily habit. Don't bite off more than you can chew; start with just a few verses each day. "Continue in what you have learned and have become convinced of, because you know . . . the holy Scriptures, which are able to make you wise for salvation through faith in Christ Jesus" (2 Timothy 3:14-15). A deeper understanding of God's Word makes it easier to know what God wants in *any* situation, because you know Him so well. Making His Word part of your thinking and decision making deepens your faith.

• **Follow instructions.** "All Scripture is God-breathed and is useful for teaching, rebuking, correcting and training in righteousness" (2 Timothy 3:16). If it's so useful, doesn't it make sense to have Scripture available in any situation? The best way to do that is to memorize it. Even Jesus, when faced with temptation in the desert, relied on the Word of God to get Him through. (See Matthew 4:1-11.) Commit with a friend to memorizing one verse a week that addresses a current struggle. For anger, try Psalm 37:8; fear, John 14:27; lust, start with Colossians 3:5. When you find your feet starting to slip, let God's Word roll off the tip of your tongue to keep you from falling.

• **Climb on.** If you are tied into the Word but still standing on the ground, you are missing the point! Second Timothy 3:17 continues, "So that the man of God may be thoroughly equipped for every good work." God didn't equip you just to look cool in your helmet and climbing harness. He wants you to climb! What does that look like in real life? It means taking risks to tell others about Jesus. It means loving and serving the people around you—even your parents and that annoying guy in your chemistry class. It means making choices that honor Him in everything from schoolwork to sports, free time to a future career.

■ **PRAY IT OUT:** *"Lord, I need You on the rock climb of life. Please make Your Word come alive."* Thank God that He hasn't left us climbing alone. Thank Him for the power of His Word, and ask Him to give you the discipline to learn it and the courage to depend on it as your lifeline.

TRIBAL MARKS

A KEY POINT I LEARNED TODAY: _____

_____

_____

_____

_____

_____

HOW I WANT TO GROW: _____

_____

_____

_____

_____

_____

MY PRAYER LIST: _____

_____

_____

_____

_____

_____

_____

SURVIVOR SECRETS

▶▶▶**WEEKLY MEMORY VERSE:** *You alone are the LORD. You made the heavens, even the highest heavens, and all their starry host, the earth and all that is on it, the seas and all that is in them. You give life to everything, and the multitudes of heaven worship you.* —**NEHEMIAH 9:6**

TRIBAL QUEST

Understand that you are not alone. Plug into the power of the Holy Spirit, your Guide, Helper, Strengthener, and Advocate sent by God to live in you and guide your life.

EXPLORE THE WORD: JOHN 14:15-21

TRIBAL TRUTH

I will ask the Father, and he will give you another Counselor to be with you forever—the Spirit of truth. The world cannot accept him, because it neither sees him nor knows him. But you know him, for he lives with you and will be in you. —**JOHN 14:16-17**

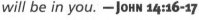

TRIBAL FACE

A Young Man in Love
JEREMY V. JONES

She was leaving, packing up all the belongings she could fit into her

Honda and moving across the country. Birmingham, Alabama, is approximately 1,300 miles from Colorado Springs, Colorado, and it might as well be on the other side of the world. I didn't know if I would see her again.

My heart felt like a caged lion, pacing back and forth inside my chest, searching desperately for a way out, a plan of attack, a weakness in the bars, anything I could do besides sit and wait and feel helpless.

Yet this had been the plan all along. I knew that she was leaving, moving away from home after graduating from college, following God's leading to new places and new lessons in her own life. Her stopover at home was only temporary. But two months was long enough for us to spend lots of time together—and for me to fall in love with this beautiful girl named Janna who had been a close friend for several years. Could it all be over so quickly?

There must be something I could do.

I stayed up late the night before her departure, journaling frantically, writing ideas and options to change her mind, and pouring out prayers and requests to God. I had sought His guidance and committed this relationship to Him from the start. I thought He had been opening doors to move forward. Could this be part of His plan? It wasn't the way I would write the script. Maybe if I showed up on her doorstep with flowers or cool music playing, she would change her mind, confess her love for me, and stay in town.

Lord, what should I do?!

I searched His Word for solace and wisdom.

"Thou shalt go to her and win her love" was the

verse I was looking for in my Bible, but I can assure you it's not there. Instead, "Wait on the Lord" seemed to echo from its pages. *There must be something else,* I thought. *You've got another message for me—right, God?*

I turned to the love chapter, 1 Corinthians 13. "Love is patient."

Still not what I wanted. Doing nothing just didn't seem to make much sense. Didn't God get it? Janna was leaving . . . moving . . . a long way away. It was now or never for a deeper relationship—or was it?

If God wasn't going to give me the right message, maybe my brother could help out. "Don't you get it?" Jason said. "Praying is the most powerful action you can take. If this relationship is part of God's will, He can work out the details."

Huh. It's good to have trusted friends who can give you solid, biblical advice. And it did seem to line up with what the Holy Spirit was already saying through Scripture and in my conscience. Maybe God was giving me His guidance all along, even if it was a little different from what I had hoped for.

Back to the journal. *Okay, God, You know what's best. You know my desires and that I don't want Janna to leave. Help me to want Your will even more. I'm choosing to trust You in this relationship, even though these circumstances don't look good. Thanks for the leading of Your Spirit. Please give me the strength to follow it.*

I didn't cause a big scene. I said good-bye to Janna and wished her the best. We agreed to trust the Lord with our futures and lay off communication for a while. My emotions screamed, "No!" But there was peace in my spirit.

One year later, I proposed marriage to Janna. She wholeheartedly accepted. She had followed the Lord's leading away and then back again, allowing Him to use the distance in between to clarify His path for us. God's guidance was good. His Spirit was trustworthy. And by surrendering my desires and following His leadership even when it didn't make sense to me, I was confident of His will when it really mattered. Looking back, I wouldn't have it any other way.

God has promised more than His help; He's provided His Helper—His living, moving Spirit within us to point to God's best. Rather than spell out every detail for us ahead, He works through relationship with us to shape our character and teach us to rely on Him.

What are you hearing from the Holy Spirit? Are you listening?

TRIBAL TRAINING

• **Know your guide.** Do you realize what—or who—you've got? Think about this. The third person of the Trinity, God Himself in His Spirit form, is living inside you. And He's not just hanging out. He's there to guide you, help you, gift you, strengthen you, comfort you, and stand up for you. Look up the following verses, and jot down what each verse tells us about the Holy Spirit's role: Mark 13:11, Luke 11:13, Luke 12:12, Acts 1:8, Romans

5:5, Romans 8:26, 1 Corinthians 6:19-20, Ephesians 1:13-14, Hebrews 2:4, and Hebrews 10:15-16.

- **Listen to His voice.** The help is there. It's up to you to use it. Philippians 4:6-7 tells us to take all our requests to God with thankfulness and that His peace will guard our heart and mind. Got a question? A problem? A difficult decision to make? A temptation to overcome? When we pray, God listens, and His Spirit often guides us by providing a sense of peace about the direction we should go, even if peace seems crazy in the midst of the circumstances. Slow down. Talk to God. Search His Word. Listen to His Spirit. Back it up with the Bible. How can you tell if it's God's voice you're hearing?

- **Double-check it with the Bible.** Jesus told His disciples, "But the Counselor, the Holy Spirit, whom the Father will send in my name, will teach you all things and will remind you of everything I have said to you" (John 14:26). Did you catch the word *remind?* God's character is always consistent. The direction from His Spirit must line up with the truth of His Word. If you think He is directing you into a choice, activity, relationship, or direction that contradicts His Word, think again. If your circumstances match up with Scripture, go for it. It's always a good idea to seek counsel from one or two mature Christians as well. They can affirm or redirect your thinking.

- **PRAY IT OUT:** *"Father, help me to hear Your voice and live by the power of Your Spirit."* Thank God for providing such an amazing Helper. Ask Him to sharpen your sense of spiritual hearing and give you guidance every day in big decisions and small ones.

TRIBAL MARKS

A KEY POINT I LEARNED TODAY: _____

_____

_____

_____

_____

_____

_____

HOW I WANT TO GROW: _____

_____

_____

_____

_____

_____

MY PRAYER LIST: _____

_____

_____

_____

_____

_____

A WARRIOR'S CALLING

KNOW HOW TO GROW
WEEK 3

SURVIVOR SECRETS

>>>**WEEKLY MEMORY VERSE:** *For the word of God is living and active. Sharper than any double-edged sword, it penetrates even to dividing soul and spirit, joints and marrow; it judges the thoughts and attitudes of the heart.*
—HEBREWS 4:12

TRIBAL QUEST

The privilege of prayer is one of the birthrights God gives His sons. No matter how hard life gets, prayer reminds you that you aren't alone or powerless.

EXPLORE THE WORD: JAMES 5:13-16

TRIBAL TRUTH

Is any one of you in trouble? He should pray. . . . The prayer of a righteous man is powerful and effective.
—JAMES 5:13, 16

TRIBAL FACE

K. P. Westmoreland—Heaven-Bound Hoopster

THUNK, THUNK, THUNK . . . SWIIIIISH!

A perfect shot.

K. P. Westmoreland retrieves the ball, bounces it off a teen's "backside," dribbles it between his legs, rolls it around his head, then throws again. *SWIIIIISH!* The South Dakota auditorium thunders with applause.

Next, this hotshot ball handler wows the crowd with an unbelievable balancing act: He spins two basketballs on his fingers, then on two long poles . . . then spins one ball on a pole while dribbling another.

Just as everybody's eyes are about to spin right out of their sockets, K. P. shoots from the heart.

"I don't have to tell you how much I love basketball," he says. "And to perform well on the court, I have to put forth the sweat and commit to knowing the game plan."

K. P. then holds up a Bible. "It's like that in life. You've got to follow God's game plan. You have to talk to Him daily through prayer. Above all, you have to listen to His direction."

The Bethany, Oklahoma, native jumps into a powerful talk he delivers to youth groups all over North America—the story about how he grew up in the church, yet tried to play by his own rules. But this time, just as he gets to the part about how drugs nearly destroyed his life, K. P. feels a tug on his heart.

He pauses and scans the crowd of teenage campers. He senses God telling him to share his darkest secret.

No way, Lord, he prays silently. *You've forgiven my past. Why bring up memories I'm trying to forget?*

K. P. wipes sweat from his forehead, then decides to continue speaking. *I'll obey You, Lord, but I don't understand.*

"I have one more thing to tell you," he says to the audience. "Something I've never told anyone. It wasn't just the party scene that nearly messed up my life. There's more.

"When I was a teen, I got a girl pregnant. We were both ashamed of what we had done and wanted to cover up our mistake. Convinced that we had only one choice to make, we drove to a health clinic. And on a very horrible day that I wish I could forget, my girlfriend had an abortion."

The auditorium is completely silent as K. P. speaks. "We didn't solve our problems—we ended a life. We made a decision that will haunt us for the rest of our lives."

K. P. wraps up his talk, telling how Jesus has forgiven him and his ex-girlfriend and how God offers the right choices. "It's up to us to obey Him and make decisions we'll never regret."

The gym thunders with applause again. K. P. forces a smile, waves, then slips into the men's locker room.

Why, God? he prays. *Why would You have me tell that story? Nobody knew except my ex-girlfriend, the doctor, and You. Why bring it up now?*

One year later, K. P. got an answer.

He returned to the same South Dakota gym to share his basketball skills with a new crop of campers. Just as the athlete had finished performing and was packing up his equipment, a 16-year-old girl tapped him on the shoulder. "Uh, excuse me," she said softly. As K. P. turned around, he noticed that the teen was cuddling a baby in her arms. "I'd like you to meet my little boy," she said. "He's just six months old."

K. P. held the child, realizing that the young mother

had gotten pregnant out of wedlock. He looked the girl in the eyes. "I'm proud of you for not making my mistake," he said. "You didn't cover up your sin with another sin. You made the right choice by giving birth to this baby."

The girl smiled. "It's all because of you," she said. "I was in the crowd last year. I sat in the back row, confused and depressed. I was thinking about getting an abortion, until I heard your story. You made me think about how abortion doesn't just end a pregnancy; it *ends a life.* I knew I couldn't do that."

The young basketball player stood speechless, staring into the face of the wriggling baby boy. Tears began to roll down his cheeks.

Thank You, Jesus, he prayed silently. *Thank You for this child. Thank You for the obedience of this incredible girl. Thank You for prayer. Thank You for faith. Thank You for eternal life.*

Imagine if K. P. hadn't connected with his Creator through prayer or obeyed the Lord's leading. That child probably wouldn't be alive today.

Through prayer, we can open a window that allows God's eternal love and healing power to shine into our lives; we can open our hands to receive His many blessings; we can open our hearts to let His presence fill and strengthen us.

In the words of R. C. Sproul, "The Lord God of the universe, the Creator and Sustainer of all things, . . . not only commands us to pray, but also invites us to make our requests known. . . . In the act and dynamic of praying, I bring my whole life under His gaze. Yes, He knows what is in my mind, but I still have the privilege of articulating to Him what is there. He says, 'Come. Speak to Me. Make your requests known to Me.' And so, we come in order to know Him and to be known by Him."[1]

God hears and answers our prayers. But we must be proactive. We must open the window by kneeling before Him in prayer. The book of James tells us that we have not because we ask not (4:2) and that the effectual, fervent prayer of a righteous man accomplishes much (5:16). Again and again, the holy Scriptures reveal to us that prayer is an effective tool.

Are you committed to prayer? Are you convinced of the power of prayer? Would your friends recognize that spending time with God is one of your core values?

TRIBAL TRAINING

• **Think back to how you became a Christian.** K. P. Westmoreland isn't the only one with a powerful testimony. Everybody who follows Jesus has a story about how the Lord used circumstances to bring him to his knees.

• **Contemplate how prayer factored into your decision to accept Christ.** Who was praying for you when you were younger? A parent? A grandparent? A Sunday-school teacher? Your attitude toward prayer may very well be a reflection of those who have modeled prayer for you.

▪ **Talk to the Lord every day.** All it takes is verbalizing your hopes and fears to the Lord throughout the day. In the middle of a test or when faced with the temptation to do wrong, admit your need to God. And then when you have a reason to feel good about life, remember to say thanks.

▪ **PRAY IT OUT:** *"Lord, I want to talk to You more often than I tend to."* Be honest with Jesus and tell Him that praying doesn't come all that easily for you. Ask Him to bring people into your life who will teach you nonchurchy ways to connect with Him.

TRIBAL MARKS

A KEY POINT I LEARNED TODAY:_____

_____
_____
_____
_____
_____
_____

HOW I WANT TO GROW: _____

_____
_____
_____
_____
_____
_____

MY PRAYER LIST:_____

_____
_____
_____
_____
_____
_____

SURVIVOR SECRETS

>>>**WEEKLY MEMORY VERSE:** *For the word of God is living and active. Sharper than any double-edged sword, it penetrates even to dividing soul and spirit, joints and marrow; it judges the thoughts and attitudes of the heart.*
—**HEBREWS 4:12**

TRIBAL QUEST

Train spiritually. Build spiritual strength and learn to discern God's will by spending time daily in the Scriptures.
   EXPLORE THE WORD: 1 CORINTHIANS 9:24-27

TRIBAL TRUTH

Everyone who competes in the games goes into strict training. They do it to get a crown that will not last; but we do it to get a crown that will last forever.
—**1 CORINTHIANS 9:25**

TRIBAL FACE

Chris Caruana—*Breakaway* **Athlete**
   Go out for track? Who—ME?!
   Chris Caruana thought his parents were being absurd when they suggested he take up the sport, or any sport for that matter. See, he's a

thinker, a dreamer, an artist, and a musician—not an athlete. Yet his parents insisted that he give the sport a try, you know, as a way to mold him into a well-rounded student. So he accepted their challenge, even though he was terribly skeptical.[1]

At some point along the way—during one of his intense training regimens, in fact—Chris had a strange encounter: He actually found himself enjoying track.

Though the practices were grueling and the first meet was one of the hardest experiences of his life, Chris soon discovered that he had much more potential as an athlete than he imagined. Best of all, he began to make some amazing faith connections with the sport.

Our spiritual "race" requires endurance, and we can get this kind of strength only from the Lord. In track, Chris strived to improve and sharpen his abilities in order to do his best. Likewise, in our faith journey, we must deepen our wisdom and strive to grow closer to God. The apostle Paul said it this way: "Do you not know that in a race all the runners run, but only one gets the prize? Run in such a way as to get the prize" (1 Corinthians 9:24).

Chris also realized that the discipline required in track is similar to the discipline necessary in his relationship with God. Before every meet, his team warmed up together and then ran a lap. If they weren't disciplined about doing this, they'd risk cramping up or pulling a muscle.

"We need to train hard spiritually, as well. How? Prayer and Bible study. Working out daily with the Word helps us avoid getting hurt in life," Chris says.

Paul recognized the same need for discipline long ago and wrote, "I beat my body and make it my slave so that after I have preached to others, I myself will not be disqualified for the prize" (1 Corinthians 9:27).

Perhaps the most exciting lesson is this: The more we train our spirit, the more in tune we become to our heavenly Coach. Throughout the season, Chris and his teammates followed the directions of their coach. As they did so, they began to understand what he expected of them. They recognized his purposes, developed trust in his character, and saw the fruit of following his methods. The same is true in our spiritual lives. The more time we spend with God studying His Word, the more skilled we become in understanding His guidance.

"The Lord empowers us to do what's right, and He steers us clear of trouble—if we tune in to His instruction," Chris says. "True, we don't always like the path God puts us on, but He is the ultimate Coach. If we're serious about our faith, we do our best to obey Him."

Like Chris, we all need to strive to maintain a consistent, steady pace through the race of life. For those who run with Christ, the ultimate finish line is much greater than a gold medal or cash prize; it is the reward of eternity with God. Imagine the exhilaration of finishing strong, breaking the tape, and hearing this praise from our Creator, Father, and Coach: "You ran the good race. Well done, My faithful servant."[2]

Are you spiritually fit, or is your faith a bit flabby around the middle? How is your daily discipline of spending time in God's Word?

• **Go For the goal.** Training doesn't just happen. You must set a goal and work toward it. In what areas of faith do you need to grow? What results do you want to see in your relationship with God? Based on your answers, make a specific plan for the next month. Make it realistic but challenging. Choose a book or books of the Bible to read. Decide how much time each day you'll spend reading the Bible. Write it down.

On your mark. Get set. Go!

• **Tally your training log.** Where are you in your relationship with God right now? What are your struggles? What are your questions? Be honest. Write them down. Keep your notes. Look back after a week or a month of following your training regimen and see how you've grown and how God is revealing Himself to you through His Word. Update your questions and keep persevering.

• **Join a team.** "Therefore, since we are surrounded by such a great cloud of witnesses, let us throw off everything that hinders and the sin that so easily entangles, and let us run with perseverance the race marked out for us" (Hebrews 12:1). Training is tough, physically and spiritually, but accountability from team-mates can keep you going. Tell a friend or two about your plan. Or better yet, make a plan together. Check on each other to see how things are going. Create a system of consequences for falling short and rewards for following through.

• **Play with power.** Don't underestimate the force of Scripture. Hebrews 4:12 tells us, "For the word of God is living and active. Sharper than any double-edged sword, it penetrates even to dividing soul and spirit, joints and marrow; it judges the thoughts and attitudes of the heart." Expect it to come alive as the Holy Spirit makes it real and uses it to transform you from the inside out.

■ **Finish strong.** "You were running a good race. Who cut in on you and kept you from obeying the truth?" Paul asked (Galatians 5:7). People stop training or quit in the middle of an actual race for various reasons: fatigue, injuries, distractions. Have you made a commitment like this before and quit along the way? Don't let that stop you from trying again. List the obstacles that might hinder you and ways to combat them in the future.

• **PRAY IT OUT:** *"Lord, please give me the discipline to build spiritual strength."* Thank God for His Word as a guide for your life. Ask Him to bring the Bible alive. Ask Him to give you perseverance and endurance.

TRIBAL MARKS

A KEY POINT I LEARNED TODAY:_____

_____

_____

_____

_____

_____

_____

HOW I WANT TO GROW: _____

_____

_____

_____

_____

_____

_____

MY PRAYER LIST:_____

_____

_____

_____

_____

_____

_____

SURVIVOR SECRETS

For the word of God is living and active. Sharper than any double-edged sword, it penetrates even to dividing soul and spirit, joints and marrow; it judges the thoughts and attitudes of the heart. —**HEBREWS 4:12**

TRIBAL QUEST

Meditate: Focus on the truth and power of God's Word. Wrestle with the questions it raises in your everyday life.

EXPLORE THE WORD: PSALM 119:96-112

TRIBAL TRUTH

To all perfection I see a limit; but your commands are boundless. Oh, how I love your law! I meditate on it all day long. Your commands make me wiser than my enemies, for they are ever with me. —**PSALM 119:96-98**

TRIBAL FACE

Breakaway Brian—New Meditator
Meditation is weird, something people from other religions do, sitting cross-legged, chanting. Besides who can sit still for that long anyway? Brian thought.[1]

DAY 17: MEDITATE ON THE MESSAGE

But he couldn't get past his youth pastor's words: Meditation is in the Bible, lots of places, and something "God wants us to do. Consider it a spiritual brain exercise: focusing and thinking through specific sections of Scripture."

His youth pastor recommended trying John 13:1-17, so Brian opened his Bible and read the passage like he would any other book. It was the story of the Last Supper; it looked interesting but it didn't seem much different from a book he might read in history class. Brian began to read it again with greater care, focusing on sentences, words, characters, and scenes. A phrase jumped out at him. He wasn't completely sure what it meant but it stuck in his mind: "Having loved his own who were in the world, he now showed them the full extent of his love" (John 13:1). As he continued thinking about it, something started happening inside Brian's imagination:

"Have a seat, Brian," Jesus said, motioning to an empty seat near the end of the low wooden table.

Brian glanced around his surreal surroundings. Several men nodded, and one handed him a piece of unleavened bread. *That must be John next to Jesus,* he thought. *And Judas! Do the others know what he's about to do?!* He sat on cushions near the end of the table.

The room seemed earthy and dark. The flames of oil lamps cast dancing shadows on the adobe-like walls. The men seemed comfortable together, but there was a tension in the air.

Jesus sat in the middle of the men, fully bearded, tan, and

wearing a coarse robe. Brian couldn't take his eyes off Jesus, and yet he could muster only quick glances at His eyes. It wasn't that he didn't want to. Brian felt drawn to Jesus' deep brown eyes. They gave Brian a sense of love mixed with the deepest sadness, but there was also a piercing strength that scared him. The feeling made him want to run far away from Jesus and directly into His arms all at the same time. For now, it was all the young guest could do to sit speechless and try to comprehend this complex scene.

The men grew quiet as Jesus stood, removed his outer robe, and wrapped a long, narrow towel around His waist. He stepped toward Andrew, who appeared confused and uncomfortable as Jesus knelt, dipped the towel in a water basin, and cradled Andrew's heel in His hand. Gently, He massaged Andrew's left foot, then right, with the moistened towel. The towel removed the dirt from the crowded city streets, which were a mixture of dust, mud, and animal excrement. The coating of filth from the disciple's feet muddied the water in the basin.

Why is He doing this? Brian thought. Apparently the other men had the same question. Several of them exchanged puzzled glances, and Brian heard one or two muffled whispers. All the while, the men kept their eyes on Jesus as He moved from one man to the next, repeating the cleansing process.

When Jesus moved to Peter, the stocky man pulled his feet away and questioned Jesus: "Lord, are You going to wash my feet?"

"You do not realize now what I am doing, but later you will understand," Jesus replied, looking up and capturing Peter's gaze. The two locked eyes for a long moment. It seemed to Brian as if a silent mental wrestling match were taking place behind Peter's stare.

"No, You shall never wash my feet," Peter protested, but his resolve seemed to be weakening with each millisecond, his eyes dropping to the floor even as he spoke.

Jesus sighed. His words came firmly yet patiently, "Unless I wash you, you have no part with Me."

Peter leapt to his feet, nearly kicking over the wash basin. He threw his arms into the air, practically shouting, "Then, Lord, not just my feet but my hands and my head as well!"

Brian inched forward. Everything within him surged upward, ready to jump up with Peter and cry, "Me, too!" But he felt anchored to his seat. Seconds ticked by but seemed like eternity. The sound of Peter's anxious breath sounded like a roar.

Jesus broke the silence with a low chuckle, and He motioned toward Peter's seat. "That's not necessary, Peter," Jesus told him. "I've already cleansed you completely, so I need to wash only the surface dirt." Peter sat down, his countenance a mixture of sheepish relief. Brian thought the disciple's eyes looked a bit teary.

The mood remained solemn as Jesus repeated the washing process around the room. Jesus knelt in His tunic, pouring water over crusty feet, wiping away the grime with His own cracked and rugged hands, drying with the coarse towel. Occasionally Jesus would smile at the man in front of Him, though most of the time He seemed meditative, prayerful perhaps. Brian was transfixed with the scene that seemed to play out in slow motion.

Before he knew it, Jesus was kneeling in front of Brian. Though he had witnessed the process 12 times, he thought there was some mistake. *Me, Jesus?! These others are Your disciples. I—I'm just a boy from the twenty-first century!* His thoughts and emotions swirled like a tornado. He felt blood rush to his head as the gaze of 12 men plus Jesus focused on him. His mouth felt dry. *No, wait, surely I don't belong here. I, wait—*

A peace deeper than any he'd felt flooded Brian as Jesus' hands lifted his foot and poured the cool water over his toes. Though the fibers of the towel were rough, Brian felt only a gentle soothing. He knew he did not deserve this kindness and he longed to trade places, kneeling and washing the feet of Jesus instead. Humility bathed his spirit.

Jesus was done. He stood, wiping His hands. "Do you understand what I have done for you?" He asked the men. "Now that I, your Lord and Teacher, have washed your feet, you also should wash one another's feet. I have set you an example that you should do as I have done for you. I tell you the truth, no servant is greater than his master, nor is a messenger greater than the one who sends him."

Brian jumped, startled by the ringing phone. He didn't move to answer it. Instead, he knelt and prayed, "God, I think I get it."

"No servant is greater than his master," he repeated out loud as he wrote it on a scrap of paper. He would read it periodically throughout his day and dwell on the message he had learned. It would become a part of him.

That's the point of meditation. It's the active, thoughtful contemplation of the truths of God's Word or reflecting on God and the person and work of Jesus Christ. It is a powerful, though often ignored, tool for Christians to use along with prayer and Bible reading.

Are you ready to sharpen your mind and let the power of Scripture transform you?

TRIBAL TRAINING

• **Meditation defined.** Philippians 4:8 tells us to "think about" whatever is true and pure, using the Greek word *logizomai,* which means to take inventory of—or to think through something as if it were a mathematical problem. The opposite of meditation is "mental flight," allowing your brain to run away from the hard work of concentrating on Scripture. Biblical meditation is not, as some Eastern religions teach, an emptying of your mind for the purposes of relaxation or other self-serving and ungodly results. Meditation is rightly linked with peace, but that peace is rooted in God Himself and the truth of His Word.

• **Meditation demanded.** Meditation is commanded by God. "Be transformed by the renewing of your mind. Then you will be able to test and approve what God's will is—his good, pleasing and perfect will" (Romans 12:2). Following God's commands brings about the desire in Christians to obey, and letting God's Word shape our thinking generates the ability to understand God's will. Sometimes God's truths may seem hard to grasp, but consider the examples of Daniel (Daniel 7:28) and Mary (Luke 2:19, 51). Both faced situations in which they couldn't figure out what God was doing, but instead of giving up mentally, they did their best to ponder and carefully consider their situations.

• **Meditation directed.** Find a quiet place where you won't be disturbed. Read a passage of Scripture—Psalms is a great place to start—and think through every word. Ask questions: *What do specific words mean? Do I act like these people? How can I obey this command in real life?* Turn your questions and answers into prayers. Write the passage of Scripture and carry it with you. Read it and think through it during the day.

• **PRAY IT OUT:** *"Lord, please bring Your Word alive within me."* Thank God for His written message to us. Ask for discipline to study it. Ask Him to let it shape your spirit and thinking.[2]

TRIBAL MARKS

A KEY POINT I LEARNED TODAY:_____

_____

_____

_____

_____

_____

_____

HOW I WANT TO GROW: _____

_____

_____

_____

_____

_____

_____

MY PRAYER LIST:_____

_____

_____

_____

_____

_____

_____

SURVIVOR SECRETS

▶▶▶WEEKLY MEMORY VERSE: *For the word of God is living and active. Sharper than any double-edged sword, it penetrates even to dividing soul and spirit, joints and marrow; it judges the thoughts and attitudes of the heart.*
—**HEBREWS 4:12**

TRIBAL QUEST

Confess your sins and be restored to a right relationship with God.
EXPLORE THE WORD: 1 JOHN 1:5-10

TRIBAL TRUTH

If we claim to be without sin, we deceive ourselves and the truth is not in us. If we confess our sins, he is faithful and just and will forgive us our sins and purify us from all unrighteousness. —**1 JOHN 1:8-9**

TRIBAL FACE

The Criminal on the Cross

Three rough-hewn wooden crosses stood starkly on a desolate hill. The ever-darkening sky swept down upon a motley crowd, painting an ominous backdrop to the rocky, arid landscape.

"Liar! Lunatic!" a voice croaked and wheezed. Its owner gasped for breath, wincing at the crushing weight upon his chest. "Aren't You the Christ?" he jeered. "Save Yourself and us—if You can!" This criminal knew death was imminent: The sticky blood running from his palms and the gathering gargle of fluid in his throat served as constant reminders. Sweat dripped off his nose. His eyes rolled in his head like a crazy man's, yet he gathered enough hatred to focus them on the man hanging beside him. "Even a son of the devil could call demons to save him!" he spat. "But You . . . are . . . nothing—"

"Enough!" snapped another criminal. "Even in the face of death, you are a fool!" The man struggled to catch his breath. "Don't you get it? Don't you fear God? We are punished justly, for we are getting what our deeds deserve. But this man has done nothing wrong."

The second criminal turned to the third man who hung in the middle of the conversation. Sweat stung the second man's eyes as well, but now he felt another burning as tears began to flow. A new weight had been pressing down on him, growing heavier as this day wore on. The nearer he came to his end, the more rapidly the visions flowed: victims, targets, innocents. Their faces haunted him now, each adding an unseen stone to the crushing weight in his soul. Despite his tremendous physical suffering, he would double it if he could, just to be rid of this anguish within.

Yet tormented as he felt, he somehow sensed a greater weight upon the man dying next to him. He had read the placard above the man's cross: "This is the King of the Jews." Though meant as a mockery, the message echoed within this criminal's mind. All day he had watched soldiers and members of the crowd hurl insults and abuse. "If You are really the Christ, save Yourself!" they sneered. "He saved others but can't save Himself," they cackled. Yet rather than curse back, the man responded in prayer, "Father, forgive them, for they do not know what they are doing."

The convict had heard the stories about this Jesus, the tales of healings and miracles. Hadn't He even stood up for the outcasts and accused? Surely this prophet did not belong here, dying between two notorious lawbreakers.

A glimmer of hope pierced his pain and a flood of remorse broke loose within him. His whole life became suddenly clear, focalized in the present moment. He knew he would die; it was unavoidable and approaching quickly. Yet this innocent man—no, God—beside him was his only possibility for freedom, for forgiveness. Never had he wanted something so great. He had nothing left to lose.

"Jesus!" he sobbed desperately. "Jesus! Remember me when You come into Your kingdom!" His body slumped forward from the effort, and he felt the nails pinch and tear in his flesh. His chest heaved. He wept and struggled for breath, longing for Jesus' response, knowing he deserved none.

Jesus' breath was labored also, but His reply clear, "I tell you the truth, today you will be with me in paradise."

The words reverberated to the criminal's core. Love he had never known filled and cleansed him. His sobs continued to shake his body, but now it seemed the

tears washed him. A strange peace—could it really be joy?—enveloped him. Death grew nearer and nearer, but now it brought no fear. As long as he could muster strength, the criminal would keep his eyes fixed on this Jesus, source of his new life, Savior of his soul.

Three men, condemned to die, suffered through their final agonizing moments on earth. Two were guilty, but one was innocent, dying to take away the sins of the world. Even in the process of His death, Jesus teaches us powerful truth.

How often are we like the first criminal? We do something wrong and find ourselves facing the consequences. We want Jesus to prove Himself, to save us from the situation we are in. We want Him to get us down off the cross, but we don't want to admit that we deserve to be there. We listen to the enemy's lies, condemning us, pushing us down under the suffocating waters of guilt. *What would you say?* the subtle voice says. *He doesn't want to hear it again. Don't you remember what you did?* Instead of asking for and receiving the grace of Jesus Christ, we stubbornly hold on to our pride. Like the first criminal, we lash out in anger against our only source of hope. We clutch hungrily to our sin, allowing shame to drive us away from our source of forgiveness.

But the second crucified criminal provides us a beautiful example of the power of confession. Casting aside pride, standing against shame, he admits his sin, acknowledges Christ's innocence, and asks Jesus to remember him once He is reunited with the Father. It's simple, straightforward, and honest—just like confession.

His example shows us how easy it is to experience life and its freedom over death and its condemnation. Jesus had no lectures waiting. He did not dissect the prisoner's sins or give second thought to His response. Instead, He offered acceptance and cleansing, love and comfort, and freedom on the deepest level possible.

The consequences of the nameless man's sins were not erased, and God does not remove the natural reactions from our actions. But just as this criminal met his end with a peace and certainty more powerful than death, so can you face your circumstances with strength, freedom, and guidance from God's Spirit. God's grace is available. Reach through the darkness and grasp His light.

Are you ready to be completely honest, laying your deepest sin in the open before Jesus? Are you ready to experience the freedom that comes from confession?

TRIBAL TRAINING

- **Live in the light.** Place a plant in a really dark place for a few days. Leaves that were once thriving and vibrant grow limp and droopy and brown without light. Your spirit is the same. "If we claim to have fellowship with [God] yet walk in the darkness, we lie and do not live by the truth. But if we walk in the light, as he is in the light, we have fellowship with one another, and the blood of Jesus, his Son, purifies us from all sin" (1 John

1:6-7). Too often we allow our shortcomings, sins, and the resulting condemnation from the devil to cover us with a blanket of darkness. Are you growing spiritually? If not, are you choosing sin over Christ? Are you listening to the lies of darkness rather than the light of truth?

• **Shake off shame.** Throw off the stifling blanket of shame. Tell Jesus what's on your heart and mind. Confession isn't just being sorry you got caught; it's admitting you have done wrong and need forgiveness. First John 1:9 says, "If we confess our sins, he is faithful and just and will forgive us our sins and purify us from all unrighteousness." Did you catch those key words: *faithful, forgive,* and *purify?* God knows your every thought and action already, so forget about feeling embarrassed. Be real and let Him do His work of freedom within you.

• **Find fellowship.** "But if we walk in the light, as he is in the light, we have fellowship with one another, and the blood of Jesus, his Son, purifies us from all sin" (1 John 1:7). Likewise, James 5:16 says, "Therefore confess your sins to each other and pray for each other so that you may be healed." Don't underestimate the power of accountability. Is there a friend you can talk to about the sin you're struggling with? What about a youth pastor, parent, or other trusted adult who can encourage you to continue walking in the light? Walking together is a valuable part of living in the light. Think of someone today whom you will ask to encourage and challenge you in your faith on a regular basis.

• **PRAY IT OUT:** *"Lord, I confess _____ to You today. Please forgive me, purify me, and help me to live in the* *light."* Thank God that He is faithful even when you are not. Ask Him to forgive you and to help you change your actions, so that you live in a way that is pleasing to Him.

TRIBAL MARKS

A KEY POINT I LEARNED TODAY:_____

_____

_____

_____

_____

_____

HOW I WANT TO GROW: _____

_____

_____

_____

_____

_____

MY PRAYER LIST:_____

_____

_____

_____

_____

_____

SURVIVOR SECRETS

▶▶▶**WEEKLY MEMORY VERSE:** *For the word of God is living and active. Sharper than any double-edged sword, it penetrates even to dividing soul and spirit, joints and marrow; it judges the thoughts and attitudes of the heart.*
—**HEBREWS 4:12**

TRIBAL QUEST

Worship is much more than what you do on Sunday morning at church. It has to do with the way you think and the way you act.

EXPLORE THE WORD: PSALM 150

TRIBAL TRUTH

Yet a time is coming and has now come when the true worshipers will worship the Father in spirit and truth, for they are the kind of worshipers the Father seeks.
—**JOHN 4:23**

TRIBAL FACE

Johann Sebastian Bach—Committing His Art to the Almighty

You most likely own or have heard a CD of classic worship songs. But what you consider to be classic worship probably isn't the same as what your grandparents would.

The worship music you enjoy is more apt to resemble rock than Bach. Matt Redman and Chris Tomlin didn't compose their praise songs at a harpsichord. In all likelihood, they were strumming a guitar. Still, J. S. Bach isn't all that out of the loop when it comes to understanding what authentic worship is. Even though he lived more than 300 years ago, his faith is not as old-fashioned as you might think.

Johann Sebastian Bach was born on March 21, 1685, in what is now known as Germany. His dad was a professional musician and his brothers were quite musical. In fact, musical ability ran in the Bach family. For two centuries their name was synonymous with songs people couldn't get out of their heads. But young Johann was in a class by himself. He set a new standard for classical music.

As a young kid, Johann proved he had a special gift. He learned to play the violin, flute, oboe, and trumpet without much difficulty. But when he was nine years old, Johann's bright and beautiful world spun out of control. That was the year both his father and his mother died. Imagine how you'd feel to lose both your parents in a short period of time. Johann went to live with his oldest brother, Christoph. Fourteen years older, Christoph was married and employed as a church organist in a nearby town. The younger Bach found some relief from his emotional pain by learning to play the organ. For the next five years his brother tutored him in musical composition.

Because of his amazing abilities, Johann became a much sought-after organist. He played in cathedrals as well as in palaces. In addition to being a church organist, he was the king's personal musician. That's how his original compositions became so famous.

Johann introduced what he wrote to the public by playing his music instead of other people's music. This great classical composer wrote 295 cantatas and 260 chorales, not to mention his many preludes, fugues, concertos, and sonatas. Perhaps only George Frideric Handel, who was born three weeks before Bach, has the same kind of following of musicians of that era.

Johann was raised in the church, and he experienced personal faith early in his life. Because he attended Lutheran churches, he was exposed to the teaching of Martin Luther, who said that everything a person does can be an act of worship to God. For Bach there was no separation between secular and sacred. He saw writing music for the king and writing music for a church choir as equally important. Both were opportunities to use his God-given gift to express his love of life and love of God.

Writing music was an act of worship for Bach. In fact, if you look at copies of his original manuscripts, you see something very interesting. There are initials beside his name. Sometimes you see J. J., which stands for *Jesu juva* (Latin for "Help me Jesus"). More often you see S. O. G., which stands for *soli Deo gloria* (Latin for "To God alone be the glory").

When Bach died at the age of 65 in the summer of 1750, he had made a big impact on the world of music. But even more than that, his attitude about worship left a mark on the Christian world that is still visible three centuries later.

Now, you may not appreciate a Bach concerto, but that's beside the point. What you do enjoy may actually be a means by which you can enjoy God and express your gratitude for being His son. Can surfing be a way to worship? Sure. Boogie boarding? Absolutely. You can worship God by writing poetry, running, or flying model airplanes. The key is being aware of God and thinking about Him while going about the things you enjoy. In fact, approaching God worshipfully is possible in every area of life.

Once Jesus carried on a conversation with a woman who'd been living a lie through multiple relationships with men. He could see the emptiness in her life. He knew that she hadn't discovered how to live her life with an awareness of God's presence. That incident is found in the fourth chapter of John's Gospel. That's where Jesus says we worship God in spirit and in truth. In other words, worship involves experiencing God throughout the day no matter what we're doing, as well as thinking about Him and singing to Him when we are in church on the weekend.

In spirit and in truth. In church and at school. On Sunday as well as Monday. Get it? Is that an empowering thought to you?

TRIBAL TRAINING

• **Focus on God as your primary audience.** The word *worship* means recognizing the worth of something or someone. Worship starts by factoring God's presence into everything you do and remembering your life is more about Him than about you.

• **Honor God's worth by doing your best.** By writing his initials on his musical score, Bach reminded himself that what he was composing was not just to please others. He was ultimately writing for God's enjoyment. To that end he gave it all he had. We should approach what we do in such a way that it wouldn't bother us to see God's name attached to it.

• **Spend time with God every day.** Even though you can worship God as you walk to class or play your tuba in the school band, setting aside quiet time to read His Word and think about how it applies to your life is important too.

Think about the words you sing at church. Even though worship songs are only a small part of what it means to worship God, they are important. So when you are in church, don't just feel the music; focus on what the lyrics are saying and sing them directly to the Lord.

• **PRAY IT OUT:** *"Jesus, I'm glad I don't need to be a musician to be a first-class worshiper."* Ask God to help you recognize His presence as you go about your daily routine. And as you get ready for church, ask Him for a heart of true worship so that you'll be more concerned with pleasing God than with how your voice sounds to those around you.

TRIBAL MARKS

A KEY POINT I LEARNED TODAY:_____

_____

_____

_____

_____

_____

_____

HOW I WANT TO GROW: _____

_____

_____

_____

_____

_____

_____

MY PRAYER LIST:_____

_____

_____

_____

_____

_____

_____

SURVIVOR SECRETS

▶▶▶**WEEKLY MEMORY VERSE:** *For the word of God is living and active. Sharper than any double-edged sword, it penetrates even to dividing soul and spirit, joints and marrow; it judges the thoughts and attitudes of the heart.*
—**HEBREWS 4:12**

TRIBAL QUEST

Seek out Christian friends with common goals and values so you can find fulfillment in your faith adventure.
EXPLORE THE WORD: PROVERBS 27:1-10

TRIBAL TRUTH

Do not forsake your friend and the friend of your father, and do not go to your brother's house when disaster strikes you—better a neighbor nearby than a brother far away. —**PROVERBS 27:10**

TRIBAL FACE

Three Iron-Willed Bikers

As his high school graduation drew closer, Peter Frost of Wheaton, Illinois, grew increasingly excited. It wasn't just the thought of being done with classes and going through the commencement ceremony. It was more than the party and presents he knew his parents were planning. There was something else. Something he'd been planning for two years: a bike trip from coast to coast.

The strong athlete, who was mature for his age, convinced two friends from school to join him: Dan Fernandes, 17, a fellow senior from West Chicago, and 16-year-old Karl Brorson, a sophomore from Naperville.

None of the guys had done anything like this before. It was an adventure most cyclists only dream about—and it would prove to be an adventure that would test their friendship.

Although they initially toyed with biking from Washington State to Washington, D.C., the boys revised their route when they came to terms with the treachery of the Rocky Mountains. The route they settled on would take them from California to Georgia—a total of 2,700 miles. Based on their best guesses, it would take nearly a month.

On June 3, 2001, the day after graduation, the guys set off. Each biker had $400 cash, access to a cell phone, and the names of a handful of contacts along the way who would help them find a place to sleep. The three packed up their bikes, said good-bye to their families at Chicago's Midway Airport, and flew to San Diego. Once in Southern California, they rode to the nearest beach and dipped the rear tires of their bikes into the blue Pacific Ocean. The adventure had started. They wouldn't be satisfied until they were able to dip their front tires into the salt water of the Atlantic.

Wasting no time, the three headed their Trek 520

touring bikes in an eastward direction, pedaling uphill through the long and winding road through the San Bernardino Mountains. Without a stretch of level ground, they were totally exhausted by the time they'd clocked 50 miles. They decided to call it a day.

After a few days of roadside camping, the boys cruised into Phoenix—and dry beds and hot showers at Karl's uncle's place. But the one night they'd anticipated staying there turned into two. Each bike got a flat tire within the first hour as the boys attempted to ride out of Phoenix the next day. "We were so discouraged," Peter recalls. "But that setback proved to be a good thing. It gave us the chance to review our priorities for the rest of the trip."

Before leaving Chicago, the trio had agreed to three goals—sort of a biker's creed: (1) Grow closer to the Lord by learning to depend on Him more, (2) be a witness to those they met, and (3) grow in their leadership abilities by taking turns with strategy and navigational decisions.

"Until we were humbled by the flat tire fiasco in Phoenix, we had begun to focus primarily on the ride instead of relying on the Lord," Karl remembers. "It's amazing how He can use little things like flat tires as a way of helping you put life into perspective."

In eastern Arizona, the guys got word that a church in Stafford would like them to take part in their Sunday evening service. In return, the congregation would provide them a place to stay and as much as they wanted to eat. A retired insurance man at the Stafford church that evening took particular interest in the boys' expedition. The stranger gave them two $50 bills to buy spare

tires, tubes, and steak dinners. In addition, he contacted 15 people between New Mexico and Georgia who opened their homes to the boys.

Because of the size of Texas (and serious headwinds), it took Peter, Dan, and Karl nine long days to make it across. They encountered temperatures in excess of 115 degrees (which melted one of their CD players) and were introduced to humidity that they'd never known before.

The boys also had to deal with their share of maintenance and mechanical issues with their bikes. The flats in Phoenix were only the first of many. And then there were the challenges of physical exhaustion and frayed emotions that would test their friendship.

"We determined early on that we would not allow anything that bugged us to fester into a problem," Peter recalls. "We knew it was just going to be the three of us for a month and that we couldn't afford not to work things out with each other."

That determination to not sweat the small stuff, combined with a determination to laugh a lot, paid off. Though there were a few times when a bike's fork got bent, in terms of their friendship, nobody's nose got bent out of shape.

On June 30, 27 days after pedaling out of San Diego, Peter, Dan, and Karl reached Brunswick, Georgia. According to their pretrip itinerary, they were right on schedule. As they pedaled to the beach where the waves of the Atlantic surrendered to the white sand, each boy dipped the front tire of his bike into the surf as a symbolic way of saying "mission accomplished."

Imagine how those three felt as they fulfilled their dream. It must have been awesome. But it wasn't just the rush they felt having reached their long-distance destination. They were in touch with a deeper sense of fulfillment. They'd grown in their ability to trust God in hard situations and they'd also bonded as brothers.

There are friends and then there are friends. Even though you may never find yourself biking across the country, the road of life is dangerous and lonely without companionship. We all need to know we aren't journeying into the future by ourselves. We all need the kind of friends we read about in Proverbs 27:10.

What friends do you have who share your common values? Who are those whom you could call on when your dreams have gone flat and you don't have a spare? What might God be saying to you about your attempts at Lone Ranger Christianity? Remember, even the Lone Ranger had Tonto.

TRIBAL TRAINING

• **Make Friendship a priority.** God didn't create us to make it on our own. He knows the kinds of mountains that stand in our way and the predictable spills we inevitably have trying to cross over them. He wants us to have companions on the trail. In Ecclesiastes 4:9-12 the Bible says, "Two are better than one, because they have a good return for their work: If one falls down, his friend

can help him up. But pity the man who falls and has no one to help him up! Also, if two lie down together, they will keep warm. But how can one keep warm alone? Though one may be overpowered, two can defend themselves. A cord of three strands is not quickly broken."

- **Be selective in whom you spend your time with.** While friends are a prerequisite to a fulfilled life, wrong friends can be poison. Invest time and energy in friends who bring out the best in you. We become like those with whom we hang around. If you think your current "band of brothers" causes your Father to frown, ask Him to lead you to some who are part of His family.

- **Work through issues that come between you.** Friendship is a playing field in which we can put into practice the principles of love, acceptance, and forgiveness that Jesus taught. Disagreements and unresolved conflicts can lead to time-consuming detours. By talking things out, the three bikers refused to let misunderstandings slow their progress.

- **PRAY IT OUT:** *"Lord, I want friends who will help keep me headed in the right direction."* Ask the Lord for help in being a thoughtful and trustworthy friend. Ask Him to bring into your life a couple guys who will be life-long soul friends.

TRIBAL MARKS

A KEY POINT I LEARNED TODAY:_____

_____

_____

_____

_____

_____

_____

HOW I WANT TO GROW: _____

_____

_____

_____

_____

_____

_____

MY PRAYER LIST:_____

_____

_____

_____

_____

_____

_____

SURVIVOR SECRETS

>>>**WEEKLY MEMORY VERSE:** *For the word of God is living and active. Sharper than any double-edged sword, it penetrates even to dividing soul and spirit, joints and marrow; it judges the thoughts and attitudes of the heart.*
—**HEBREWS 4:12**

TRIBAL QUEST

When it seems like your prayers are bouncing off the ceiling, that's the time to keep talking to a God who really is listening.

EXPLORE THE WORD: PSALM 22

TRIBAL TRUTH

My God, my God, why have you forsaken me? Why are you so far from saving me, so far from the words of my groaning? O my God, I cry out by day, but you do not answer, by night, and am not silent. —**PSALM 22:1-2**

TRIBAL FACE

King David's Prayer—"Gimme a Break!"

You've heard of *The Prayer of Jabez*, right? That little book by Bruce Wilkinson has sold more than 30 million copies. It's based on a prayer in the Bible (1 Chronicles 4:9-10) in which a guy by the name of Jabez boldly asked God to give him a successful life. If you've read the book, you know the outcome. God answered his gutsy prayer.

But what happens when God doesn't give you exactly what you want? What about when He doesn't answer at all? Do you quit praying? Or if you keep talking to God, do you resort to telling Him what you think He wants to hear instead of what you really feel? Too many Christians have a view of prayer that keeps them from speaking out when life is caving in.

There's another guy in the Old Testament who prayed a gutsy prayer. He didn't ask God for a million bucks. No, what made his prayer courageous was the fact that he was totally honest with God even though he felt he'd gotten a raw deal from the Almighty. You could call it the prayer of "Gimme a Break." It's found in Psalm 22 where King David basically said, "Gimme a break, God. Look what You allowed to happen to me. How could You be so cruel? How could You be so far away?"

David was concerned God had forgotten all about him. In David's frontline battle to maintain control of his kingdom, the Creator of the cosmos was missing in action. No "Prayer of Jabez" answers here. In fact, there were no answers at all to the king's prayers. God was silent and His actions seemed so unfair. All the same, in this pessimistic psalm David offers us some suggestions about how to pray when we really don't feel like it.

When David prayed Psalm 22 he was in deep weeds. The happy days he'd experienced earlier in his life were a distant memory. This day was bleak because of people who were out to get him. He wasn't sure he'd live to see tomorrow.

No doubt you know what it's like to be on the ropes. Friends betray. Pets die. Parents divorce. You get cut from the team. The girl you like starts going out with someone else. And in the midst of it all it seems as if God's lost your e-mail address.

Life on a defective planet is marked by setbacks like these. David learned to expect them. So should we. The episode that prompted Psalm 22 was only one of many in the king's life. But in reading the passage did you notice that even though David is convinced that God has abandoned him, he doesn't quit praying? Not at all! In fact, he continues to pour out his heart to a God he isn't quite sure is listening to him. He acts on what he knows is true even when he doesn't have much evidence.

One of the marks of a growing Christian is the determination to look toward the Son even when He seems to be hidden by dark clouds. That's called faith.

Another mark of maturity is honesty. David is secure enough in his friendship with the Lord to be totally honest with his feelings. Isn't it kind of cool that he wants God to know he's disillusioned and jaded? Can't you just hear him? "Gimme a break, God. Life has gotten pretty lousy. Where has trusting You gotten me anyway?" Okay, so he doesn't exactly say that. But David does pray despite how he feels. Another amazing thing about this psalm is that while David is pouring his heart out in honesty, he is so aligned with God's will that he is also prophesying about Jesus (see verses 7, 8, 16, and 18).

If you haven't yet, be sure to read through all of Psalm 22. Compare the way David starts with the way he ends. By the time David has finished unloading on God, his perspective has changed. God is back in view. David is on His side.

Talk about doing a 180. It sounds like someone else on his knees. The dark clouds are gone. The sky is clear. Feelings of being forsaken have been forgotten. David is back on track with God.

It's hard to know how much time David's prayer represents. Chances are, the prayer that is recorded in Psalm 22 wasn't prayed in one sitting (or kneeling). The time between what was going on at the beginning of the prayer and at the ending could have been weeks or months. But it is likely that David kept talking to God about his situation the whole time.

In other words, hang in there. Don't give up on God just because the landscape hasn't changed overnight. It may take longer than you think. But, then again, as may have been true for David, simply telling God about your problems may help you see things about the Lord that you've forgotten. Like David, take stock in how God answered your prayers in the past.

The bottom line? Honest communication with God is a great way to process what is going on in our lives. It's a healthy way to work through what we're feeling, as well as to confide our worst fears and prized hopes to the Lord. "Gimme a break" prayers verbalize the grunt-hard difficulties and disappointments of life. When we pray them we're reminded there is no situation we face that

God is not interested in.

Perhaps you're feeling abandoned by God right now. If not now, you likely will in the near future. In an imperfect world, hurtful things will park in front of our hearts and God will sometimes seem absent. When's the last time you felt like your prayers were bouncing off the ceiling? When are you tempted to tell God what you think He wants to hear instead of what you really feel? Learn from David. God can handle what you really think.

TRIBAL TRAINING

- **Keep praying even when God seems absent.** Talk to the Lord every day. Long speeches aren't necessary. Remain in contact with the One you've committed your life to. Act as though He's listening even though you can't tell He is.

- **Don't fake it when you talk to God.** When you feel shortchanged by God, don't pretend you like it. Talk it out. Tell Him how you feel: abandoned, misunderstood, or taken advantage of. The Lord can handle whatever it is you're feeling inside. He won't be put off by what you say. The fact that David's prayer is in the Bible means God wants us to communicate our deepest doubts and raw anger even if we feel He's let us down big time. (And just in case you've forgotten, the Lord is capable of reading our minds and knows if our pious words are for real.)

- **Be patient when you pray.** God always answers our prayers. Sometimes He says yes. Sometimes He says no. And sometimes He says wait. In fact, a lot of the time He lets us wait. It's a way our faith muscles grow stronger.

■ **Think back to times God proved Himself to you.**
You know, those times when He came through and left
little doubt that He was aware of your situation. Spend
some time thanking Him for those indisputable evidences
of His faithfulness.

■ **PRAY IT OUT:** *"Lord, give me the faith to keep talking
to You when I feel like You're not listening."* Tell the Lord
you're grateful you can be totally honest with Him. Ask
Him to help you remember the times He's come through.

TRIBAL MARKS

A KEY POINT I LEARNED TODAY:_____

_____

_____

_____

HOW I WANT TO GROW: _____

_____

_____

_____

MY PRAYER LIST:_____

_____

_____

_____

A WARRIOR'S CALLING

KNOW WHICH WAY TO GO!
WEEK 4

SURVIVOR SECRETS

>>>**WEEKLY MEMORY VERSE:** *Brothers, I do not consider myself yet to have taken hold of it. But one thing I do: Forgetting what is behind and straining toward what is ahead, I press on toward the goal to win the prize for which God has called me heavenward in Christ Jesus.*
—**PHILIPPIANS 3:13-14**

TRIBAL QUEST

Even when it means relating to people who are different from us, Jesus wants us to tell others about Him.
EXPLORE THE WORD: ACTS 17:16-34

TRIBAL TRUTH

Therefore go and make disciples of all nations, baptizing them in the name of the Father and of the Son and of the Holy Spirit, and teaching them to obey everything I have commanded you. And surely I am with you always, to the very end of the age. —**MATTHEW 28:19-20**

TRIBAL FACE

Paul's Radical Mission

Paul couldn't believe his eyes. There were shrines, temples, and altars everywhere. The entire city was an interactive museum of pagan religions.

Paul had heard about the ancient city of Athens ever since he was a kid growing up in Tarsus. He knew of its mythological gods Zeus and Medusa and the rest. He'd read the writings of Plato and Socrates, Athens' most celebrated philosophers. He'd visualized Athens' famous Olympic Games. But this was Paul's first time to the city and he was wide-eyed with amazement.

His purpose in visiting the seaport city was to tell non-Jewish people about Jesus. But in all honesty he was also looking for a safe place to hide out. Just days before, this outspoken apostle had been run out of another town in hostile reaction to his message. He'd left in such a hurry, his traveling companions Si and Tim were forced to stay behind to take care of business.

Paul felt lonely as he walked Athens' main streets and alleys on his own. He sent word to the village in northern Greece for his buddies to catch up with him as soon as they could. But in the meantime, Paul couldn't help but drink in what he saw. *This is so pagan!* he told himself. *It may be pagan, but it points to an interest in spiritual things.*

Paul paused at an outdoor café to sip an espresso and reflect on what he was seeing. As he sat there he couldn't help but hear the locals talking among themselves. Their conversation was about truth and happiness and the fear of death.

Just as I thought, Paul mused. *These Athenians have a God-shaped hole in their hearts. They need to know about Jesus.*

The afternoon sun felt good on Paul's arthritic shoulder as he ordered a second espresso. Just then he heard a loud voice coming from down the street. It sounded like someone giving a speech. And then there was a loud crowd noise. People were sounding their approval. There was clapping and cheering.

When he finished his coffee, Paul paid his tab and walked down the ancient cobblestone street in the direction of what appeared to be a public rally. He rounded a corner and . . . eureka! There before him was a crowd of about a hundred people standing at the base of a white marble hill. A solitary man stood on top of the elevated ridge that served as an entrance to the world-famous Parthenon.

Paul listened to the man speaking. He looked around and tried to figure out what this gathering was all about. Within a few minutes the man on the hill came down and another person in the crowd climbed up and began speaking. Then when he was done, another took his place.

Out of the corner of his eye, Paul spotted a hand-painted sign. "Welcome to Mars Hill. This marketplace of ideas is open to all. The only currency accepted in this market is candid opinions you are prepared to debate."

The sun began to dip toward the western horizon, but the crowd didn't move. Paul decided he would take advantage of the chance to speak what was on his mind. He'd come to Athens to spread the Word as Jesus had commanded His followers in the Great Commission. This seemed an ideal opportunity.

Paul started up the slippery marble slope and stumbled. A few people laughed at the older man's misstep. But Paul found his feet and dusted off his robe. He began with the obvious.

"This is my first time to be in your fascinating city," Paul continued. "I'm blown away by the number of religious artifacts everywhere. Athens is the most religious place I've ever visited. You have altars and shrines on nearly every street corner. The Parthenon in back of me was built as a temple to your goddess Athena. I want to applaud you on your search for truth."

Paul wanted to somehow find a way to make a case for following Jesus, but he wasn't quite sure how to lead into that. And then he had an idea.

"I noticed this afternoon you have an altar to the unknown god. Well, let me be so bold as to tell you I know that god and He has a name."

Paul continued to tell them about Jesus and what He did by coming to earth, dying on the cross, and coming back to life again. His decision to tell the Athenians the good news about God's love by making reference to what they were familiar with was obviously a God-thing. He thanked the Lord for putting those thoughts in his head.

But judging from the hisses and boos that greeted Paul's remarks as he slowly climbed down the hill, he knew he hadn't made a lot of points. Still, as he started to walk toward the center of town a handful of people who'd been in the crowd approached him.

"What you talked about is very interesting," one man in the crowd said. "Several of us would like to find out more about this Jesus you mentioned. When can we get together?"

It's not hard to imagine the sequence of Paul's varied

emotions. First, he felt the rush of excitement as the Holy Spirit gave him a creative idea of how to bridge from the unknown God to Jesus. Then he was humiliated by being rejected by the masses. What a downer! But then came the unexpected request to hear more about his Lord and Savior.

Have you ever been put down when you stood up for Jesus? Has anyone ever seemed responsive when you spoke out about what God's done in your life? There is nothing quite like the thrill of being used by the Lord to draw someone you care about in His direction.

If you look for ways to share your faith, you've graduated from basic Christianity to the advanced track. Those who are willing to tell others about Jesus are those who take His Word seriously. But the truth is, it isn't all that hard if you accept the fact that not everybody will be interested.

TRIBAL TRAINING

• **Look for ways to witness for Christ.** Keep your eyes and ears open for those who seem thirsty to know more about God. People won't believe in Jesus until they're ready, so don't force the issue. Ask the Lord to give you a sensitivity to those in your sphere of influence. You'll be able to sense when they are willing to talk about faith stuff.

• **Be a natural witness.** Take your cues from the courtroom. A witness simply tells what he's personally experienced when called on. That's it. Nothing more. Take your cues from Paul. In Athens the apostle found common ground. Do the same with those you want to reach. Do your best to explain what Christians believe by relating it to values they think are important or needs you know they have.

- **PRAY IT OUT:** *"Lord, help me to see my friends the way You see them."* Ask Jesus to open your eyes to the hurts and struggles that hide behind your friends' laughter. Tell the Lord each day that you are ready and willing to talk about Him when it seems appropriate.

TRIBAL MARKS

A KEY POINT I LEARNED TODAY:_____

_____

_____

_____

HOW I WANT TO GROW: _____

_____

_____

_____

_____

MY PRAYER LIST:_____

_____

_____

_____

_____

SURVIVOR SECRETS

>>>**WEEKLY MEMORY VERSE:** *Brothers, I do not consider myself yet to have taken hold of it. But one thing I do: Forgetting what is behind and straining toward what is ahead, I press on toward the goal to win the prize for which God has called me heavenward in Christ Jesus.*
—PHILIPPIANS 3:13-14

TRIBAL QUEST

Live out in the open as a witness for Christ in every part of your life. Answer God's calling to be salt, light, and a good-smelling fragrance that attracts people to Him.

EXPLORE THE WORD: 2 CORINTHIANS 2:12-17

TRIBAL TRUTH

But thanks be to God, who always leads us in triumphal procession in Christ and through us spreads everywhere the fragrance of the knowledge of him.
—2 CORINTHIANS 2:14

TRIBAL FACE

Vince Flumiani—Creative Witness

Vince Flumiani is amped. Darting around the Jedidiah Boardriding warehouse, he gestures at stacks and racks of surf-, snowboard-, and skate-inspired products: T-shirts galore, endless hoodies, and edgy new sketches and designs everywhere. Jedidiah, the board-riding company he founded in 1999, has taken off. And Vince himself can hardly believe it.

After running away from home in high school, getting hooked on drugs, and ending up in a juvenile detention center, Vince's life was transformed when he met a family who introduced him to Christ.

His journey was just beginning. Vince joined a church, started surfing "hard-core," went to college, moved to San Diego—and found an unlikely mission field of his own: the beach. As Vince got involved in the lives of other surfers, he saw the negative impact of the culture on people searching for peace and love.

Vince knew he had to act. One morning while he was spending time with God in a coffee shop, the idea hit: *I'll form my own board-riding company.* Then he stumbled on the word *Jedidiah* while translating the Old Testament book of 2 Samuel from Hebrew for a seminary class. The meaning? "Beloved of God." It was the perfect name. Jedidiah Boardriding was born.

The logo and idea took off. Everything from the boards to the clothing line are top-notch. Most have logos with messages intended to get surfers, snowboarders, and skaters to start wondering about Christ without even realizing that's what they're doing. But Vince and his friends wanted to do more than just create cool products.

The product "is just a front," Vince acknowledges. "At the end of my life, the last thing I want to be known for is a fashion designer. I want to build a financial base to do ministry. I want to encourage people to get closer to God."

His heart, and the company's true effort, lies with the board riders with whom he and his friends build relationships. Many of the surfers, skaters, and snowboarders sponsored by Jedidiah have earned their reputations by solidly living out their Christian lives as they learn to love others and love God, effectively changing the world around them.

Vince doesn't stop with the people he backs. He's found that Jedidiah has given him an in with boarders everywhere. "When I go to skate parks and appear in lineups with other surfers, they talk to me about church and say, 'Christians are hypocrites; I won't go there.'"

So Vince goes to them, hangs with them, hurts with them, and learns their stories. He even creates products that will appeal to their tastes, hoping they'll question Jedidiah's message and wonder about the peace he's found.

"That's my passion," Vince says. "We're not a Christian clothing company—we're a board-riding company that's about Jesus Christ. We know God's never failed us. He's given us something better, and that's what I want to tell everyone."[1]

Do you think surfers and skaters can smell Vince coming? Probably not—though we really don't know much about his bathing habits. When Paul says we're to be the aroma of Christ, he's using a metaphor to describe the kind of effect we should have on others around us.

The sense of smell is powerful. Think about it: Merely catching a whiff of homemade chocolate chip cookies, a freshly cut Christmas tree, clean laundry, or a particular perfume can immediately trigger a flood of memories and emotions. Suddenly you're a kid again running to the kitchen to lick the beaters while Mom bakes. Or you're back in study hall trying to get up the nerve to talk to a girl you like.

God wants the way we live to trigger a response within others. He wants our love lived out to influence those who don't know Him. You can't see spiritual belief any more than you can see fragrance. But your presence as a follower of Christ should pack a punch that makes people perk up and wonder: *Wow. What's so fresh about his life?*

How do you smell? Are you living for Christ in every area of your life? Are those around you drawn to God because of your actions, purpose, and love for others?

TRIBAL TRAINING

• **Pick your passion.** God has called each of us to use our interests and abilities to reach others for Him in *every* area of life: school, work, family, sports, band, you name it. You don't have to form a board-riding company to reach out. But you do need to identify your gifts and commit them to God. Start by making a list of your skills and passions. It shouldn't be hard; often your passions pick you. What do you like to do? What are you good at? Ask for input from family and friends. Offer these talents to God, and ask for His guidance in using them for His glory.

• **Smell check.** Sometimes it's tricky to truly love others through the activity you enjoy. Fortunately, just as you can improve at playing saxophone, you can improve at honoring God in the jazz band. Ask yourself what kind of aroma you are putting off. Others are good at reading your true intentions. Amazing soccer skills might be obvious, but if you are cussing at opponents and putting down teammates, you aren't spreading the fragrance of God. Just like deodorant won't truly cover a really stinky sweat, a little God-talk won't cover a heart that isn't true. Ask God to make your motivations pure.

• **Do your part and let God do His.** Sometimes following Christ is discouraging. You might do everything right to share the love of Jesus with people, only to see them reject God, and maybe even you. Don't give up. Second Corinthians 2:15-16 says, "For we are to God the aroma of Christ among those who are being saved and those who are perishing. To the one we are the smell of death; to the other, the fragrance of life." You can't control other people's sniffers or whether they ultimately accept or reject Christ. But you can be faithful to live your witness in a real way and trust God to do His work in the hearts of those around you.

• **PRAY IT OUT:** *"Lord, please make me a good-smelling fragrance that draws people to You."* Thank God for creating you with unique interests, abilities, and passions. Ask Him to guide and embolden you to live for Him in every situation, and to reflect His love and saving grace through you so that others may know Him.

TRIBAL MARKS

A KEY POINT I LEARNED TODAY: _____

_____

_____

_____

_____

_____

_____

HOW I WANT TO GROW: _____

_____

_____

_____

_____

_____

_____

MY PRAYER LIST: _____

_____

_____

_____

_____

_____

_____

SURVIVOR SECRETS

▶▶▶**WEEKLY MEMORY VERSE:** *Brothers, I do not consider myself yet to have taken hold of it. But one thing I do: Forgetting what is behind and straining toward what is ahead, I press on toward the goal to win the prize for which God has called me heavenward in Christ Jesus.*
—**PHILIPPIANS 3:13-14**

TRIBAL QUEST

Run the race of faith following the example of Jesus, who was willing to endure suffering in order to finish strong.

EXPLORE THE WORD: HEBREWS 11:32–12:3

TRIBAL TRUTH

Let us fix our eyes on Jesus, the author and perfecter of our faith, who for the joy set before him endured the cross, scorning its shame, and sat down at the right hand of the throne of God. Consider him who endured such opposition from sinful men, so that you will not grow weary and lose heart. —**HEBREWS 12:2-3**

TRIBAL FACE

Todd Beamer—"Let's Roll!"
Where were you on September 11, 2001, when you heard about hijacked jets flying into the World Trade

Center in New York City? Perhaps you were in your home-room at school. Maybe you were eating breakfast or about to catch the bus. It's possible you stumbled down the stairs half-awake and caught your folks staring at the television in tears.

Todd Beamer was on United Airlines Flight 93 when he heard. This 31-year-old computer software salesman was on a business trip, en route to California from New Jersey. About an hour into the flight, Todd and the other passengers knew that something was terribly wrong. A couple of men had stormed the cockpit, attacked the pilot and copilot, and taken over the controls. Two other hijackers herded Todd and the other passengers to the back of the plane as it started to fly erratically.

Passengers next to Todd made calls on their cell phones to tell friends or loved ones what was going on. That's when those on Flight 93 (including Todd) first heard about "Ground Zero."

Todd tried to call his wife but couldn't get through. Instead, using the Airfone in his seat, he called an opera-tor and asked her to convey his love to his wife if any-thing should happen to him. In addition, he also asked the woman on the other end of the line if she would pray the Lord's Prayer with him.

Todd first learned that prayer as a preschooler. His parents raised their son to understand that God gives us what we need—a day at a time, moment by moment. So Todd knew at an early age that the Lord's Prayer is some-thing to be prayed in times of crisis. (God actually invites us to ask for His help when we feel surrounded by evil.)

Todd's parents modeled what it meant to trust God

for daily decisions—especially how to act like Jesus. Even though "W. W. J. D." bracelets hadn't yet become popular, Todd was always encouraged to ask himself, "What would Jesus do?"

Of course, Todd's parents are the first to admit that their son wasn't exactly a perfect saint. There were times during Todd's adolescence when he really didn't want to roll out of bed on Sunday mornings and go to church, yet his mom and dad insisted he go. There were times he talked back to his parents, but as he grew older, he recognized they really loved him and wanted him to grow up to make a difference in the world. There were even times when he lost his temper and said things he shouldn't have. But during those times, Todd remembered that Jesus died on the cross for people who weren't perfect. His pastor remembers Todd as being a kid who wanted deep down to live his life for his Lord.

After graduating from high school in 1987, Todd went on to nearby Wheaton College, where he pursued a degree in business. His love of sports was challenged by his love for a spunky, blonde-haired classmate named Lisa. It didn't take Todd long to decide which was more important.

Following graduation, Todd and Lisa were married and moved to New Jersey where he worked for Oracle (a leading computer software company). They had two sons (David and Drew) and were expecting their third child when Todd left for California on that unforgettable Tuesday in 2001.

Knowing that terrorists had already flown planes into the twin towers of the World Trade Center, as well as the

Pentagon, Todd began to piece together the likely scenario when Flight 93 began to turn away from California and fly toward Washington, D.C.

It's very likely that he suspected that the hijackers were going to fly the plane into another national monument. Perhaps the Capitol building. Maybe even the White House. Todd probably knew that the hijackers were intent on destroying a national landmark and killing hundreds of innocent people.

Perhaps Todd knew deep inside that there wasn't much chance that he or any of the passengers would survive this horrible ordeal. Even before Todd picked up the phone to relay a message to his wife and pray with the Airfone operator, his Christian faith was observed by those around him. Although scared of what was about to transpire, Todd exhibited a Christlike desire to lay down his life for others. He stood at the back of the plane and hatched a plot with the other frightened passengers. They would rush the hijackers and take control so that the plane wouldn't crash into the nation's capital.

After all, he probably thought to himself, *that's what Jesus would do.* When Todd finished praying the Lord's Prayer and told the operator good-bye, perhaps he sensed the Lord's will was about to be done on earth as it was in heaven.

He turned to the other guys around him and said, "Let's roll!" A few minutes later United Flight 93 crashed into a field in rural Pennsylvania.

Todd died the way his mom and dad had raised him. Convinced that his life belonged to Jesus and that he was guaranteed of going to heaven, he laid down his life for the sake of others. The courage he displayed before he died was rooted in a faith that was planted in his heart as a preschooler. Chances are, God has used your family or your friends to guide you in your Christian walk. He's made an investment in your life because He wants to use you to make a difference in your world.

How might you build on the foundation of faith others have poured into your life? What are some ways you might stand up for what you believe today? It's in the little choices we make that God can use us in a big way. Don't chicken out and play it safe. Stand up and be counted.

TRIBAL TRAINING

• **Establish godly patterns.** Responding the way he thought Jesus would was not something out of the ordinary for Todd. The reason he took a stand and called on God on that doomed airplane was because he spent time with the Lord regularly. He read his Bible daily and went to church weekly. Getting in shape to run the race you desire as a believer might also mean going on a missions trip to develop a strong heart that's sensitive to others.

• **Expect opposition.** It's not likely you'll ever find yourself on a hijacked jet, but you will be put in tough situations beyond your comfort zone. The apostle Peter promised we'd face tough times. "Dear friends, do not be surprised at the painful trial you are suffering, as though something strange were happening to you" (1 Peter 4:12). When we know we'll have to sprint sometimes, we learn to pace ourselves.

- **Pray with someone when you're feeling weak.** What you do when you're feeling overwhelmed indicates just how strong you really are. Todd Beamer picked up a phone onboard the plane and found courage by praying with someone else. Admitting you're weak is an indicator you're strong enough to face what's facing you.

- **Don't hold back.** Let it roll! If you are keeping your eyes on Jesus, He's your main Man. That's whom you want to please. You want to do what you think He'd do. That means being assertive. Look for ways to let your light shine. Stand up for the kid at school others tend to pick on. Volunteer to head a project in your church youth group. Don't just jog as you leg out your faith. Sprint!

- **PRAY IT OUT:** *"Lord, help me to take a stand for You no matter what the cost."* Ask the Lord to give you courage for what you will face today. Ask Him to let you make a difference in the world around you.

TRIBAL MARKS

A KEY POINT I LEARNED TODAY:_____

_____

_____

_____

_____

_____

_____

HOW I WANT TO GROW: _____

_____

_____

_____

_____

_____

_____

MY PRAYER LIST:_____

_____

_____

_____

_____

_____

_____

SURVIVOR SECRETS

>>>**WEEKLY MEMORY VERSE:** *Brothers, I do not consider myself yet to have taken hold of it. But one thing I do: Forgetting what is behind and straining toward what is ahead, I press on toward the goal to win the prize for which God has called me heavenward in Christ Jesus.*
—**PHILIPPIANS 3:13-14**

TRIBAL QUEST

Break out of the comfort of your spiritual bubble. Get real about radically obeying Christ.

EXPLORE THE WORD: JOHN 15

TRIBAL TRUTH

My command is this: Love each other as I have loved you. Greater love has no one than this, that he lay down his life for his friends. You are my friends if you do what I command. —JOHN 15:12-14

TRIBAL FACE

Mike Yankoski—Homeless Christian
The bedraggled figure stirred slightly, trying to shake the sound that echoed as if from far away. But there it was again: "You can't stay here. Time to move on!" This time

the voice penetrated his sleep more clearly and the groggy young man half opened his eyes. The reality of another day on the streets came sharply into focus.

As he rolled over on the concrete patio that had been his bed for the night, the stench of body odor rose out of his three-dollar, thrift-store sleeping bag. Sticks, leaves, and other debris clung to his long, matted hair. Dirt and grime from months on the streets clung to every pore and crease of skin. How long had it been since he'd had a shower? The thunderstorm he'd been caught in several days ago didn't count.

He leaned against the metal railing that had served as his headboard and placed a hand on the guitar case lashed to it. He was happy the instrument was still there—and that no one had assaulted him in the night. *Maybe my singing will bring in enough change for a decent meal today,* he thought. *And if I hurry, I might be able to get hot coffee and biscuits at a shelter before they run out.*

His former life seemed so distant now: loving parents and a sister in a small town near Denver; a comfortable home where basic needs such as food, water, shelter, and plumbing lay at his fingertips; his own Land Cruiser to go wherever whenever; a solid church; friends and studies on the beautiful campus of Westmont College in Santa Barbara, California. Sometimes even he could not believe that he had left all that behind and chosen to live homeless.

The thought flickered in Mike Yankoski's head during a church sermon one Sunday: *Be the Christian you say you are.*[1]

He had driven 20 minutes to reach the church building past a world that needed him to do just that, and he would drive past again back to his comfortable life on a Christian college campus. The student struggled to remember a time when he had needed to lean fully on Christ rather than rely on his own abilities.

"The idea came instantly—like the flash of a camera or a flicker of lightning. It left me breathless, and it changed my life," Mike wrote in his book *Under the Overpass.* "What if I stepped out of my comfortable life with nothing but God and put my faith to the test alongside of those who live with nothing every day?"[2]

The concept seemed crazy, but the dream was born. The theology/computer science student discussed his desires with his parents, his pastors, and the directors of homeless ministries. The group of mature Christians became his advisers and helped him in researching and planning his adventure. Because life on the streets is dangerous, Mike found a partner to join him, another student named Sam Purvis.

Together the two entered the world of the downtrodden, taking no money and few supplies, nothing but their meager packs and guitars. For six months, they lived on the streets of six American cities: Denver; Washington, D.C.; Portland, Oregon; San Francisco; Phoenix; and San Diego. Why? Because they had heard a still, small voice saying, "Follow Me." Because they wanted "to understand the life of the homeless in the

United States and see firsthand how the Church is responding to their needs." Because they wanted "to encourage others to 'live out loud' for Christ in whatever ways God is asking." Because they wanted to grasp "what it means to depend on Christ for daily physical needs and to experience contentment and confidence in Him,"[3] no matter how much or little they had.

Mike and Sam's journey led them among the lives of the broken, hurting, and addicted. As the pair's physical appearance was worn down and altered outwardly, their outlooks and perceptions were transformed inwardly. Every morsel of food, every safe moment, every compassionate encounter brought genuine thanksgiving to God. The young men witnessed the destructive power of the devil in human lives and the unconditional love of God for each of His human creations. They understood what it meant to be shunned by society and were able to offer the touch of Christ to those accustomed to human rejection. They came to understand at their core the need and appreciation of Jesus as their rock, the foundation of their lives.

At the end of six months, Mike and Sam were able to walk off the streets and return to "normal" life as you and I know it. But their experiences on the streets and their new perspectives in their journeys with God will forever shape them.

"God probably isn't calling you to live on the streets like He did Sam and me," Mike wrote. "But He is calling you—like He does each of His children—to take important risks of faith that are unique to you and your opportunities. Your journey will lead you toward utter dependence on the King of kings and a resolution to follow Him wherever He may ask you to go. That might be to the streets, to your friends and family, to your neighbor, or to a stranger you haven't even met yet."[4]

Dare to live a life abandoned to God. Dare to love and live radically. Dare to obey the command of Christ in Matthew 16:24-25: "If anyone would come after me, he must deny himself and take up his cross and follow me. For whoever wants to save his life will lose it, but whoever loses his life for me will find it."

In the words of Mike Yankoski, college student and former homeless man, "Walk off the edge with Him."[5]

TRIBAL TRAINING

• **Identify your mission.** "What are the new steps of faith God is asking you to take today—steps that may feel like you're going off the edge of the known world for Him?" Mike wrote in his book, "Who are the people God has placed in your life that He is calling you to notice, to reach out to, to share His love with?"[6]

• **Love the least.** "Then the righteous will answer him, 'Lord, when did we see you hungry and feed you, or thirsty and give you something to drink? When did we see you a stranger and invite you in, or needing clothes and clothe you? When did we see you sick or in prison and go to visit you?' The King will reply, 'I tell you the truth, whatever you did for one of the least of these brothers of mine, you did for me'" (Matthew 25:37-40). The starving, the poor, the sick, the imprisoned: Jesus calls us to care for them. What about the unpopular students in your school? How can you love them?

• **Realize risk.** Who said following Jesus would be safe? Who said it would bring fame or comfort? "All men will hate you because of me, but he who stands firm to the end will be saved," Jesus told His followers in Matthew 10:22. "Blessed are you when people insult you, persecute you and falsely say all kinds of evil against you because of me," He said in Matthew 5:11. Jesus' teachings turned the world upside down in His day. They continue to contradict what our culture—and sadly sometimes even our Christian culture—tells us is important and worth striving for. Want to be great? Be a servant (Matthew 20:26-27). Want to represent Christ? Love others (John 13:34-35). Dare to take your faith beyond a T-shirt or bracelet slogan and meet the real needs of real people in real ways.

• **PRAY IT OUT:** *"Lord, give me new boldness to obey Your commands."* Thank God for His detailed care and concern for the lowliest of His creation. Confess your questions, doubts, and fears. Ask Him to revolutionize your thinking and provide opportunities to serve Him in real ways.

TRIBAL MARKS

A KEY POINT I LEARNED TODAY:_____

_____

_____

_____

_____

_____

HOW I WANT TO GROW: _____

_____

_____

_____

_____

_____

MY PRAYER LIST:_____

_____

_____

_____

_____

_____

_____

Week 4: KNOW WHICH WAY TO GO!

SURVIVOR SECRETS

>>>**WEEKLY MEMORY VERSE:** *Brothers, I do not consider myself yet to have taken hold of it. But one thing I do: Forgetting what is behind and straining toward what is ahead, I press on toward the goal to win the prize for which God has called me heavenward in Christ Jesus.*
—**PHILIPPIANS 3:13-14**

TRIBAL QUEST

When you're tempted to give in to your natural instincts, walk in the Spirit instead.

EXPLORE THE WORD: GALATIANS 5:16-23

TRIBAL TRUTH

So I say, live by the Spirit, and you will not gratify the desires of the sinful nature. —**GALATIANS 5:16**

TRIBAL FACE

Laying Down Everything For Jesus

It was a cloudy, drizzly summer morning. Rich stood over his brother's grave. As he wiped the warm mist from his face, he thought about the last time he'd heard Erik's voice.

Nine months earlier, the two of them had gone to their high school football game. With two minutes to go in the fourth quarter, they decided to leave since their team was ahead by two touchdowns. They laughed as they walked side by side from the stadium to the parking lot. Erik kidded his older 18-year-old brother that one of the school's varsity cheerleaders had turned Rich down when he'd asked her out the previous weekend. Rich gave Erik a brotherly shove to the shoulder.

Before reaching their car, the boys were ambushed by a handful of thugs. The colors they wore indicated they attended the crosstown rival school whose team was losing. The bullies demanded money. When Erik reached for his wallet, Rich told him to stop. He let the intruders know what they could do with their demand and then proceeded to push the apparent leader of the gang.

At that, one of the group came at him with an aluminum baseball bat. Rich saw the shiny weapon in time to duck. But his 14-year-old brother didn't. Whack! The sound of metal hitting a human head triggered fear in Rich. It also caused the gang of no-gooders to turn tail and run.

"Erik!" Rich shouted, reaching down to his brother who lay in a pool of blood. He looked into his little brother's face hoping for some indication that he had just been knocked out and would recover. What he saw, however, offered no hope at all. Erik's eyes were open but unresponsive. He was dead.

Within three hours the runaway teens had been apprehended by police. That, however, was little consolation to Rich and his parents, who stumbled through the reality of Erik's death in a state of shock and intense grief. Within a few months the one who'd taken the fatal swing with the bat was convicted and sentenced to two years in a juvenile detention facility 50 miles away. But that brought little relief to Rich and his parents.

As Rich walked away from Erik's grave, he wiped a tear from his cheek. Gosh, he missed his little brother. Even though they were almost four years apart, they had been best friends. Starting the car and driving away from the cemetery, he thanked God his sadness was not compounded by hate and revenge.

Oh, he'd felt all three emotions for a while. For two months Rich was unable to focus at school. His grades dropped and his appetite evaporated. Each weekend he drove around aimlessly. Even though he was a Christian, he started making a list of what he could do to get even with those in the gang who had killed Erik. His list included such things as slash tires, kill a family pet, and spray graffiti.

He carried his feeble excuse of a list around in his pocket. But he didn't take it all that seriously. Even if he were able to get away with his plan, it wouldn't bring Erik back. One Sunday at church Rich was touched by something his pastor said. The sermon was based on Matthew 25 where Jesus said that those who visit prisoners are actually visiting Him. Out of the blue, Rich pictured the face of the kid who had killed his brother behind bars.

"No way, Jesus," Rich prayed silently. "There's no way I would ever forgive that punk for what he did. You wouldn't expect me to do that, would You, Lord?"

But as he continued to listen to the sermon, it

dawned on him. The Lord wasn't just asking if he'd be willing to forgive Erik's assailant. He was asking him if he'd be willing to visit the killer in prison as a way of illustrating he'd forgiven him.

As Rich left church, there was a knot in his gut. He knew he had to forgive the scum. How could he? There was no way. After all, he had a right to carry a grudge, didn't he? But lying on his bed that night, Rich stared at the ceiling. In the pitch darkness he asked the Lord for the ability to do the most difficult thing he'd ever had to do. And then he heard a voice. "Jesus, I forgive him for killing Erik." It was his voice. Somehow God had given him the power to let go of his intense hatred.

Two weeks later Rich graduated from high school. The very next day he drove to the prison and visited some-one he had killed in his thoughts multiple times over the previous nine months. The boy recognized Rich as he walked into the visitation room. His face betrayed the fear he felt. But within 10 minutes, that face was stained with tears as Rich told him he'd forgiven him for what he'd done.

Sound impossible? Perhaps. Offering forgiveness to someone who doesn't deserve it and hasn't asked for it isn't natural. But, hey, as a Christian you've been given a supernatural power. It's called the Holy Spirit. Through the Spirit you can get your eyes off what seems unfair and focus them on what God desires. In the Spirit you have the ability to serve others and not just yourself.

- **Don't believe everything you feel.** Feelings aren't always reliable. Sometimes they mislead us. A lot of the time our feelings are based on what we think is right instead of what God says is right. According to what our culture suggests, we can be justified in wanting to get even. But getting even can be at odds with what God has in mind.

- **Don't forget your purpose on this earth.** You have been given the privilege of a relationship with the Creator of the universe, and that relationship should be used to challenge the way people determine what is just, pure, and right. Accepting that assignment will likely result in being misunderstood and falsely accused as Jesus was. But it's worth it.

- **Don't rely on your own strength.** As young Americans we grow up recognizing that the Declaration of Independence helps to define our values. Unfortunately, too many Christians declare their independence from God and try to depend on their own ability to do what He wants. Peter learned that lesson the hard way. In Mark 14:27-31 he vows he will be loyal to his Lord, but in the same chapter (verses 66-72) he falls flat on his face. Once Peter relies on the Holy Spirit (Acts 2) and not on his own willpower, we see him demonstrating amazing courage.

- **PRAY IT OUT:** *"Lord, help me to live each day aware of Your power within me."* Take time to listen to Jesus before you fall asleep at night. Ask Him if there's something He'd like you to do or someone He'd like you to forgive.

TRIBAL MARKS

A KEY POINT I LEARNED TODAY: _____

_____

_____

_____

_____

_____

_____

HOW I WANT TO GROW: _____

_____

_____

_____

_____

_____

_____

MY PRAYER LIST: _____

_____

_____

_____

_____

_____

_____

SURVIVOR SECRETS

▶▶▶WEEKLY MEMORY VERSE: *Brothers, I do not consider myself yet to have taken hold of it. But one thing I do: Forgetting what is behind and straining toward what is ahead, I press on toward the goal to win the prize for which God has called me heavenward in Christ Jesus.*
—PHILIPPIANS 3:13-14

TRIBAL QUEST

Distinguish between the world's views and God's ways by viewing life through the lens of Scripture.

EXPLORE THE WORD: ROMANS 12:1-8

TRIBAL TRUTH

Therefore, I urge you, brothers, in view of God's mercy, to offer your bodies as living sacrifices, holy and pleasing to God—this is your spiritual act of worship. Do not conform any longer to the pattern of this world, but be transformed by the renewing of your mind. Then you will be

able to test and approve what God's will is—his good, pleasing and perfect will. —ROMANS 12:1-2

TRIBAL FACE

Breakaway Ryan—Confused Christian

When it came to Christian stuff,

Ryan had it together.[1] His family was solid, he could quote all kinds of verses, he was at youth group every week, and he even led a Bible study before class at his high school.

No one at church expected to hear the stories floating back from his college about first semester. He was questioning his faith, partying with friends, exploring different beliefs, and failing his classes. What happened? Was his high school faith so weak that it could crumble this quickly? Where was the Christianity he had stood on so firmly in earlier days?

The truth was that he had started to view things differently even during his high school years. The questions had crept in slowly, but Ryan had kept them to himself rather than sacrifice his image. Slowly, unresolved doubts began eroding his relationship with Christ.

Ryan's best friend in high school was a Mormon; their long talks about Jesus had raised questions he never answered, or couldn't. As he watched the news from around the world, he began to wonder if Christianity really was the only true way to salvation. What about all those people in other parts of the world? Were their religions really wrong? Were they all really going to hell? Then there was the girl he had taken to prom. She was amazing, so caring and compassionate toward others. But she didn't believe in God. She said there wasn't any absolute right or wrong; each person just had to find his own truth. He had wanted to tell her about Jesus, but he couldn't argue with her open-minded acceptance of everyone and all beliefs.

Ryan looked good on the outside, but his mind and heart were full of questions. When he hit college, his safety net of family, friends, and church community was gone. The worldviews that picked at the periphery of his thinking in high school now bombarded him front and center. He was surrounded by postmodernism, which says, basically, that "nothing hangs together—that everything is in pieces," including truth.[2] He was taught relativism, which says the same thing his prom date did: There is no absolute truth, only what is true for you.

The messages he faced overwhelmed him. His mind felt like a radio tuned to no station in particular, playing static in between whatever music or talk it picked up. Somewhere along the way, Ryan had tuned out God's voice. Now his choices left him empty and confused. Though He remained only a short, honest prayer away, Ryan felt so distant from God he didn't know where to turn.

A worldview is just as it sounds: a view of the world based on beliefs, philosophies, and understandings of what is true or not. Think of it like looking through a pair of glasses: Whatever worldview shades you wear will affect how you see and act in every area of life. Everyone ascribes to some worldview, whether or not they realize exactly what set of values and beliefs direct their thinking and actions.

None of us can escape the impact of culture. It constantly bombards us with a variety of messages, and our eyes and ears serve as radio antennae constantly receiving the signals of our society. Unfortunately, ours is a generation quick to grab on to any perspective that differs from God's Word, calling it all true in the name of tolerance as long as it feels good or gets us what we want. Much of what is broadcast—literally through TV, radio, movies, and the Internet—can undermine or over-power what biblical truth we are also receiving.

The time is now to know what you believe and why, to take the faith you've been taught maybe by your parents or at church since you were a child and make it personal. That doesn't mean ignoring your questions or hiding your doubts. It means engaging your mind with your heart, being honest with God and with fellow Christians, and searching the Scriptures for answers and real truth. It means filtering through the lenses of Scripture all the messages constantly bombarding your brain, letting God's truth continually renew your mind and transform your actions (Romans 12:2).

Sadly, Ryan's story is all too common. Don't let it happen to you. Dive into God's Word and dare to be the one to come alongside the Ryans in life, providing real love and real answers.

What do you believe and why? What questions do you have? What views of the world have you accepted as truth above the truth of God's Word?

TRIBAL TRAINING

• **Take an honest look.** What do you believe? Really. Don't just give the "this is what I'm supposed to believe" answers. Take a good, hard look at what you believe— and what your actions say you believe. Take some time to write down what you believe about God, Jesus, the Savior of the world, absolute truth, heaven, and hell. It's okay if you aren't exactly sure; just be honest. Next to each category, write down what the Bible says. If you don't know, look up some related verses, and ask your youth pastor or parents about it. As you work through your list, ask God to reveal His truth and give you the grace to believe.

• **Renew your mind.** Ever wonder what God's will for your life is? Here's a big part of how to find out: Stop conforming to the world's patterns, its worldviews and behaviors, and allow God to transform you through the renewing of your mind. "Then you will be able to test and approve what God's will is" (Romans 12:2). How do you renew your mind? It starts with reading God's Word, studying it, and focusing on His truth rather than on the ideas and philosophies of our culture. The more you know and understand it, the more you know and understand God Himself and are tuned in to His voice.

• *Sacrifice your body.* "I urge you, brothers, in view of God's mercy, to offer your bodies as living sacrifices, holy and pleasing to God—this is your spiritual act of worship" (Romans 12:1). Facing questions about what you believe is good, but God calls you to obey Him in the process. Sometimes we want to have all the answers first before offering ourselves to Him, but God wants us to do it now. Giving ourselves to the Lord through choices that honor Him is a form of worship.

• **Belong to Christ's body.** Don't forget that you're not alone. Romans 12:4-6 says that as a believer, you are part of the body of Christ. Others are there to support you, teach you, guide you, and answer your questions. Use the resources around you, and don't be afraid to be honest with others.

• **PRAY IT OUT:** *"Lord, please shape my thinking and transform me into a Christian who follows You passionately."* Thank God that He has given His truth in the Bible and through His Son Jesus Christ. Ask Him to help you recognize the worldviews that dominate today's culture and distinguish between those philosophies and His truth.

TRIBAL MARKS

A KEY POINT I LEARNED TODAY:_____

_____

_____

_____

HOW I WANT TO GROW: _____

_____

_____

_____

MY PRAYER LIST:_____

_____

_____

_____

_____

SURVIVOR SECRETS

>>>**WEEKLY MEMORY VERSE:** *Brothers, I do not consider myself yet to have taken hold of it. But one thing I do: Forgetting what is behind and straining toward what is ahead, I press on toward the goal to win the prize for which God has called me heavenward in Christ Jesus.*
— **PHILIPPIANS 3:13-14**

TRIBAL QUEST:

Ground yourself in God's Word and know what you believe.

EXPLORE THE WORD: COLOSSIANS 2:6-15

TRIBAL TRUTH:

See to it that no one takes you captive through hollow and deceptive philosophy, which depends on human tradition and the basic principles of this world rather than on Christ. — **COLOSSIANS 2:8**

TRIBAL FACE

Chuck Colson—Powerful Politico

Chuck Colson was a powerful man. Each day he came and went from the stately Oval Office, receiving assignments from President Richard M. Nixon and giving his opinions to the world's mightiest leader on a wide range of topics. As Special Counsel to the President from 1969 to 1973, Colson was a member of the President's inner circle of most trusted advisors.

When President Nixon wanted something done, he called on Colson. After all, Colson's campaign strategies had secured his election to the highest office in the land in 1968 and again in 1972. And it was Colson's hard-nosed tenacity that wrangled opponents into submission and cut through red tape.

It didn't matter to Colson that his tactics often included "dirty tricks." It was all part of the political game and maintaining the upper hand in the high-stakes game of power. If he had to leak false information to cut down an opponent or find a job for the friend of an official in order to win his vote on a key issue, so be it. This was more than a job; it was a cause that Colson believed in with religious fervor. Colson was convinced that the nation needed President Nixon, and he was willing to do almost anything for this man whom he so admired.

Colson had the respect of the President, but the press was another matter. Colson was a favorite target of criticism and was known as Nixon's hatchet man. "Incapable of humanitarian thought," said the media of the day.[1]

Although Colson didn't like being cast as a bad guy, he took pride in his position. In fact, pride had always been a part of his life. He worked hard. He had graduated valedictorian from high school, turned down a full scholarship to Harvard University to spite what he viewed as a snooty intellectualism, earned the rank of Captain in the U.S. Marines, and graduated with honors from George Washington University law school. Yes, Chuck Colson was a self-made man who had reached lofty heights where he was respected and feared by many.

Then why did his life feel so empty? Even in the moments of one of his greatest triumphs, President Nixon's 1972 reelection, Colson felt unsatisfied.

Perhaps fulfillment lay in the private sector, he thought. Colson returned to his law practice in 1973. Yet even the huge fees and high demand of a legal hotshot failed to ease the gnawing inside.

White House trouble followed Colson into private life as the Watergate scandal escalated. Shortly before the 1972 election, two men had been caught breaking into Democratic Party headquarters. As investigations followed, evidence pointed back to connections within the Nixon administration. It wasn't long before the press was implicating Colson, though he had nothing to do with this illegal activity.

During this time of turmoil, Colson encountered an old friend. Tom Phillips, the successful president of a large corporation, explained that he had entered into a personal relationship with Jesus, a relationship that had changed his life in all aspects.

This was a new concept to Colson, whose intellect and worldview told him that Jesus was merely a historical figure, great in His day but not someone whom he could relate to. But clearly Tom had changed.

Colson found himself wanting to know more about Tom's experience with God. One evening, Tom explained his story to Colson and invited him to open himself to Christ. "I can't tell you I'm ready to make the kind of commitment you did," Colson said, shaken. "I've got to

be certain. I've got a lot of intellectual hang-ups to get past."[2]

Nevertheless, Colson barely made it out of his friend's driveway before breaking down sobbing. On the roadside, one of Washington's fiercest prayed his first prayer: "God, I don't know how to find You, but I'm going to try! I'm not much the way I am now, but somehow I want to give myself to You." "Take me," he repeated over and over.[3] For the first time Colson knew that he was not alone.

The following week, Colson dug into a copy of C. S. Lewis's book *Mere Christianity,* which Tom had given him. Lewis's logical explanations of Christianity resonated within Colson's brain. By the end of the week, his mind had arrived at the same place as his heart: believing that Jesus Christ was indeed God. "Lord Jesus, I believe You. I accept You. Please come into my life. I commit it to You,"[4] Colson prayed.

But his troubles did not disappear. The press ridiculed Colson in print, and he found himself drawn into the Watergate grand jury investigation and eventually indicted. After pleading guilty to a Watergate-related charge of obstruction of justice, he was sentenced to one to three years in federal prison. Colson served seven months, which he dedicated to deepening his faith. As he grew as a new Christian, he witnessed God transforming his mind and actions.

The days behind bars were difficult, and Colson vowed never to forget the men and women still there. After his release, he founded Prison Fellowship to minister to convicts and their families. He has gone on to become one of the nation's most effective proponents of Christian worldview, hosting "BreakPoint," a syndicated radio commentary, and writing numerous books. His *How Now Shall We Live?* is one of the most clearly communicated explanations of how a Christian worldview should influence every area of a believer's life.

Chuck Colson's life is an excellent example of the difference Christ makes. Once at the top of all he viewed as important—politics, power, and pride—Colson discovered an emptiness that only Christ could fill. God met the man on his search for truth, directing him to His Son, Jesus. He answered Colson's prayer, taking him, rearranging his outlook, and using him as a powerful servant.

How is your spiritual pulse? Is your worldview rooted in God's Word? Is your relationship with Christ radically shaping your actions?

TRIBAL TRAINING

• **Question with caution.** It's okay to have questions, even doubts. There are a lot of confusing philosophies and ideas in our world. God's Word directs us to test them all: "Do not believe every spirit, but test the spirits to see whether they are from God, because many false prophets have gone out into the world" (1 John 4:1). As the source of ultimate truth, God is big enough to handle your honest seeking, and He wants to give you

His guidance as you wrestle your way to a deeper understanding of Him.

• **Pursue truth.** The key to spiritual seeking lies in your method. Check your motives and examine your emotions. Are you honestly searching for real truth? Are you trying to better understand God? Or are you trying to disprove God in order to run from Him or justify your own desires? First John 4:2-3 gives us a standard to hold to: "This is how you can recognize the Spirit of God: Every spirit that acknowledges that Jesus Christ has come in the flesh is from God, but every spirit that does not acknowledge Jesus is not from God."

• **Avoid captivity.** The teachings of Christ flip the ways of the world upside down. But our culture screams its values of selfish interest and pleasure loudly and constantly. It can be easy to let those values seep into our own ways of thinking. Remember, there is a spiritual battle raging for your mind and heart. Focus on Christ daily to keep from being taken prisoner by hollow philosophies and deceptive worldviews.

• **Know your roots.** "So then, just as you received Christ Jesus as Lord, continue to live in him, rooted and built up in him, strengthened in the faith as you were taught, and overflowing with thankfulness" (Colossians 2:6-7). It all comes back to Jesus. Let Him guide you in thinking through your faith and direct you in living out your life based on a solid understanding of His Word.

• **PRAY IT OUT:** *"Father, reveal Your truth to me and let it shape my thoughts, feelings, and actions."* Thank God for His unlimited knowledge. Ask Him to guide you in understanding your worldview.

TRIBAL MARKS

A KEY POINT I LEARNED TODAY:_____

_____

_____

_____

_____

_____

_____

HOW I WANT TO GROW: _____

_____

_____

_____

_____

_____

_____

MY PRAYER LIST:_____

_____

_____

_____

_____

_____

_____

Notes

Day 4

1. Jeremy V. Jones, "Spiritually Stoked," *Breakaway,* January 2004, p. 18.

Day 6

1. James Bryan Smith, *Rich Mullins: An Arrow Pointing to Heaven* (Nashville: Broadman & Holman, 2002), p. 172.

2. Smith, p. 150.

3. Rich Mullins, "Remember to Forget Yourself," *Campus Life,* January 1991.

4. Rich Mullins, "My One Thing." *Never Picture Perfect,* Reunion, 1986.

Day 8

1. C. S. Lewis, *They Stand Together: The Letters of C. S. Lewis to Arthur Greeves* (New York: Macmillan, 1979), p. 135.

2. C. S. Lewis, *Surprised by Joy* (New York: Harcourt, 1955), p. 172.

3. Lewis, *Surprised by Joy,* p. 226.

4. Lewis, *Surprised by Joy,* p. 228.

5. Lewis, *Surprised by Joy,* p. 229.

6. Lewis, *They Stand Together: The Letters of C. S. Lewis to Arthur Greeves,* p. 425.

Day 10

1. James Montgomery Boice, *The Sovereign God* (Downers Grove, Ill.: InterVarsity Press, 1978), pp. 141-142.

Day 11

1. Matthew 27:46.

2. Mark 16:6.

Day 12

1. Walter Wangerin, Jr., *The Book of God* (Grand Rapids, Mich.: Zondervan, 1996), p. 623.

2. Ted Miller, *The Story* (Wheaton, Ill.: Tyndale, 1986), p. 316.

3. Eugene H. Peterson, *The Message Remix: The Bible in Contemporary Language* (Colorado Springs, Colo.: NavPress, 2003), p. 1770.

4. A. Scott Moreau, *Essentials of Spiritual Warfare* (Wheaton, Ill.: Shaw, 1997), p. 51.

Day 15

1. R. C. Sproul, *Effective Prayer* (Wheaton, Ill.: Tyndale, 1984), p. 32.

Day 16

1. Adapted from Chris Caruana with Michael Ross, "Track and Faith: The Ultimate Competition," *Breakaway,* April 2005, p. 21.

2. See 2 Timothy 4:7 and Matthew 25:21.

Day 17

1. Brian is a fictional character.

2. Portions of this chapter were adapted from Mark Kakkuri, "God Wants More Meditation," *Breakaway,* May 2005, p. 29.

Day 23

1. Adapted from Betsy Holt, "Jedidiah's Journey," *Breakaway,* May 2002, p. 18.

Day 25

1. Mike Yankoski, *Under the Overpass* (Sisters, Ore.: Multnomah Publishers, 2005), p. 11.

2. Yankoski, p. 12.

3. Yankoski, p. 15.

4. Yankoski, p. 167.

5. Yankoski, p. 168.

6. Yankoski, p. 167.

Day 27

1. Ryan is based on a real teen whose name has been changed.

2. J. Budziszewski, *How to Stay Christian in College* (Colorado Springs, Colo.: NavPress, 2005), p. 45.

Day 28

1. "About Chuck Colson," Prison Fellowship, www.pfm.org, 2004.

2. Charles W. Colson, *Born Again* (Old Tappan, N.J.: Spire, 1976), p. 115.

3. Colson, p. 117.

4. Colson, p. 130.

More Great Resources
from Focus on the Family®

Tribe: A Warrior's Heart
by Michael Ross

Deep inside, you yearn for something more. You crave a life of adventure and risk—to be a hero, to be a warrior, to know the Creator intimately. Join the experience in this challenging, 28-day devotional journey that will strengthen your faith and deepen your desire to walk boldly with God!

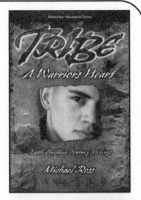

Tribe: A Warrior's Battles
A Purity Game Plan for Guys
by Michael Ross & Manfred Koehler

The battle for purity is growing increasingly difficult—but there are ways to succeed. *Tribe: A Warrior's Battles* offers young men can't-lose strategies while being on the front lines. Become God's warrior—dare to build the courage to know, serve and obey Him.

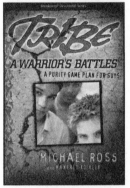

Dare 2 Share
A Field Guide to Sharing Your Faith
by Greg Stier

Sharing the gospel is the most important thing you'll ever do—and, probably one of the most challenging. So, how do you do it and where do you begin? In *Dare 2 Share*, author and speaker Greg Stier equips you with a witnessing game plan, and the information, support and confidence you need to change your world for Christ.

FOR MORE INFORMATION

Online:
Log on to www.family.org
In Canada, log on to www.focusonthefamily.ca.

Phone:
Call toll free: (800) A-FAMILY (232-6459)
In Canada, call toll free: (800) 661-9800.

Focus
on
the Family®

BP●

FOCUS ON THE FAMILY®

teen outreach

At Focus on the Family, we work to help you really get to know Jesus and equip you to change your world for Him.

We realize the struggles you face are different from your parents' or your little brother's, so we've developed a lot of resources specifically to help you live boldly for Christ, no matter what's happening in your life.

Besides teen events and a live call-in show, we have Web sites, magazines, booklets, devotionals, and novels . . . all dealing with the stuff you care about. For a detailed listing of the latest resources, log on to our Web site at **www.go.family.org/teens.**

Breakaway®
Teen guys
breakawaymag.com

Brio®
Teen girls 13 to 15
briomag.com

Focus on the Family Magazines

We know you want to stay up-to-date on the latest in your world—but it's hard to find information on relationships, entertainment, trends, and teen issues that doesn't drag you down. It's even harder to find magazines that deliver what you want and need from a Christ-honoring perspective.

That's why we created *Breakaway* (for teen guys), *Brio* (for teen girls 13 to 15), and *Brio & Beyond* (for girls ages 16 and up). So, don't be left out— sign up today!

Brio & Beyond®
Teen girls 13 to 15
briomag.com

 Phone toll free: (800) A-FAMILY (232-6459)
In Canada: (800) 232-6459